Men or machines

Situation of Capas–Botolan road

Men or machines

A study of labour-capital substitution in road construction in the Philippines

Deepak Lal

assisted by

A. Heap, H. Boisen,
B. Nilsson and L. Karlsson

International Labour Office   Geneva

ISBN 92-2-101720-6 (limp cover)
ISBN 92-2-101721-4 (hard cover)

First published 1978

Printed in Great Britain at The Spottiswoode Ballantyne Press by William Clowes and Sons Limited, London, Colchester and Beccles

PREFACE

This road construction study is the third[1] in a series of case studies, the purpose of which is to investigate the technical and economic feasibility of labour-intensive construction techniques, and to identify the institutional and policy requirements for the successful implementation of efficient techniques. It was undertaken within the framework of the Technology and Employment component of the World Employment Programme (WEP), which is financed by a generous grant from the Swedish Government.

The first phase of this study was undertaken in conjunction with the ILO comprehensive employment strategy mission to the Philippines in June–July 1973. The major conclusions of this first phase were summarised in Chapter 6 of the mission's report.[2] These conclusions were based on engineering estimates and on the derivation of a fairly comprehensive set of accounting or "shadow" prices for the Philippines which it is hoped will be of more general use and interest than some of the other parts of this study.

The second phase of the study was confined to the testing of the engineering estimates derived in Phase I by actual field experiments in the Philippines on the pilot Capas–Botolan road project. Also during this phase the World Bank kindly agreed to compare the Phase I estimates of the productivities of men and machines with their own estimates derived in part from field studies in India and Indonesia. Thus in Phase II it was possible to test the reliability not only of local engineering estimates but also of estimates based on productivity data from a different region and environment. In this second phase of the study the two Phase I ILO engineers (Hans Boisen and Alan Heap) were joined by two others, Bertil

---

[1] The two previous publications in the series are: G. W. Irvin et al.: *Roads and redistribution: Social costs and benefits of labour-intensive road construction in Iran* (Geneva, ILO, 1975); and W. A. McCleary et al.: *Equipment versus employment: A social cost–benefit analysis of alternative techniques of feeder road construction in Thailand* (Geneva, ILO, 1976). The experience gained from the case studies has been consolidated in a practical handbook prepared mainly for the use of those who are engaged in the planning, evaluation and design of road construction projects (M. Allal and G. A. Edmonds (in collaboration with A. S. Bhalla): *Manual on the planning of labour-intensive road construction* (Geneva, ILO, 1977)).

[2] ILO: *Sharing in development: A programme of employment, equity and growth for the Philippines* (Geneva, 1974).

v

Nilsson and Lars Karlsson. No changes were made in the shadow price estimates in the second phase of the study, but the various techniques were reappraised in the light of the new engineering data which emerged from the field studies of Phase II.

During the second phase an attempt was also made to examine the institutional and administrative aspects of labour–capital substitution in road construction in slightly greater detail. Information on these aspects was collected from interviews with Philippine contractors and officials in the Department of Public Highways.

This case study has various notable features. The first is the comparison of data between *ex ante* and *ex post* engineering estimates made in the Philippines. Second, the field observations in the pilot project, which covered a period of several months, also enabled the ILO engineers to experiment with modified labour-intensive methods which improved the performance of the "traditional" methods. Third, this study is a tangible example of full and active collaboration between WEP research activities and technical assistance activities. Alan Heap, who at the time was ILO/UNDP expert on construction management to the Philippine Government, not only was instrumental in getting the Government to support the WEP field study but also actively participated in its preparation and finalisation.

Two important conclusions emerge from this study. First, it *is* possible to devise technically efficient labour-intensive techniques at least for gravel road construction in the Philippines. Certain construction tasks are economically viable whether one puts market or social price tags on physical quantities. Second, in activities such as road construction it is *not* possible to transpose productivity data valid for one environment and topography into another without having detailed regard for the effect of the changes in these parameters. For example, while the World Bank Phase II study, using the Indian and Indonesian productivity estimates, found the labour-intensive methods technically inefficient, the ILO field experiments in the Philippines confirmed the hypothetical engineering estimates, thus demonstrating the technical feasibility of labour-intensive techniques.

It must be stressed that the promotion of labour-intensive methods should not be accompanied by a relaxation of accepted standards regarding working conditions. Adequate occupational safety and health measures should be incorporated at the project design stage. In particular, the relevant ILO Conventions, Recommendations and codes of practice[1] should be taken into consideration and fully implemented. Disregard of these international instruments and codes of practice cannot be justified, since it is most unlikely that labour-intensive methods would become less competitive as a result of their implementation.

The ILO wishes to thank the Government of the Philippines for permitting the ILO engineers to undertake the pilot experiments in a portion of the Capas–Botolan road. Without the generous support of the Philippine authorities and the assistance of local engineers this experiment could not have been carried out successfully.

---

[1] For the construction industry, see in particular ILO: *Safety and health in building and civil engineering work* (Geneva, 1972).

ACKNOWLEDGEMENTS

The economic research for the study was done in Manila in mid-1973, and was greatly facilitated by the ready availability of the relevant information and informants as a result of the work of the ILO comprehensive employment strategy mission. Discussions with Ajit Bhalla, Mark Leiserson, Peter Richards, Maurice Scott and Akira Takahashi were particularly helpful. Calje Falcke contributed the annex to the section on "Accounting wages" in Appendix C.

Without the expert research assistance of Franklin Meija, and the untiring and cheerful labours of a battery of National Economic and Development Authority typists in the Philippines, the economics portion of this study could not have been completed in the two months it took.

The engineering part of this study is the work of, in particular, Hans Boisen and Alan Heap, who were assisted in the field experiments by Bertil Nilsson and Lars Karlsson. They benefited from the advice and help of a large number of engineers and officials in the Philippines, as well as of the workers whose activities were monitored on the pilot Capas–Botolan project.

Information on the institutional aspects was derived during a second visit I paid to the Philippines in May 1974, and the help of various contractors, officials in the Department of Public Highways and the consulting firm of Campsax Berger is gratefully acknowledged.

The study in its final form has also benefited from the written comments of members of the World Bank Transportation Division, of Professors A. K. Sen and Howard Pack, and of G. A. Edmonds of the ILO.

To all these individuals and institutions I am most grateful.

D. L.

CONTENTS

INTRODUCTION AND SUMMARY

The purpose of this study is to answer four main policy-oriented questions:
(1) Is it feasible to find *technically* efficient labour-intensive techniques for road construction?
(2) Is the adoption of such techniques *socially* desirable?
(3) If it is desirable, what is the "ideal" system of fiscal and administrative devices to ensure that private contractors use the socially optimal technique?
(4) What are the factors affecting the large-scale implementation of efficient labour-intensive techniques?

In answering the first question it is important to remember that for technical efficiency it is imperative that any labour-intensive techniques that may be derived are not inferior—in the sense that they do not use both more capital and more labour to produce the same output. We must therefore be able to distinguish to some extent between, on the one hand, capital-biased technical progress which in a sense has been *essential* in the growth of a particular industry and, on the other, progress that has been purely the result of changing factor prices. Chapter 1 and Appendix A discuss this problem, and show why there are good reasons to believe that in product-centred industries and, in particular, in many construction tasks the technical progress which has occurred is *not* essential, and hence the possibilities of reverse technical substitution of men for machines may be technically efficient.

In Chapters 2 and 3 various techniques for building gravel roads and for particular tasks in road construction in the Philippines are described, and the results are assessed by comparing the engineering data on the productivity of men and machines with actual field experiments from a pilot road project on which the labour-intensive techniques designed by the ILO engineers associated with the study were actually used. Furthermore, the use of the World Bank data derived from field experiments in India and Indonesia has made it possible to assess the feasibility of using productivity data from one environment in another. These two sets of comparisons, as well as the estimates from field experiments, lead to the following conclusions:
(1) It is possible to devise technically efficient labour-intensive techniques (at least for certain tasks) for gravel road construction in the Philippines.

(2) It is not possible to use productivity data on men and machines from one environment in another. Moreover, any such uncritical transference can be seriously misleading. Thus, whereas the World Bank's Indian and Indonesian productivity estimates suggest that the labour-intensive techniques designed for the Philippines are technically inefficient, the actual field experiments in the Philippines generally confirmed the ILO engineers' estimates and the technical feasibility (at least in the Philippines) of labour-intensive techniques in road construction.

Technical efficiency is only one of the conditions which have to be met if labour is to be substituted for capital. It is equally important to evaluate the social desirability of adopting the alternative techniques, given the relevant social opportunity costs of the various inputs and outputs, whilst taking account of various income distributional objectives. As market prices in most developing countries are distorted, it is necessary to derive shadow or accounting prices for commodities and factors of production which represent social benefits and costs. In Appendix C of this study a fairly comprehensive set of shadow prices is derived for the Philippines. These are used to determine the social desirability of alternative techniques. It is found that in most cases the labour-intensive techniques are profitable at both shadow and market prices, the social profitability being always greater than the market profitability. It is also shown that the shadow wage/rental ratio is an important determinant of the relative social desirability of the alternative techniques and that this ratio can vary both by region and by season. Moreover, the estimates of the shadow rental rates for equipment are found to be sensitive to factors on which more hard data are required.

We also consider the question of differing gestation lags of road construction projects with alternative techniques. As we have not attempted to measure the benefits of roads in this study, only qualitative conclusions are offered. For low-quality village roads on which seasonally unemployed labour can be utilised it appears that even more time-consuming labour-intensive methods of construction may well be socially desirable. It is also emphasised that, given the possibility of spreading labour over a number of sections of a road simultaneously, labour-intensive construction methods need not necessarily involve longer gestation lags than the capital-intensive alternatives. This is one matter on which more information is required, as the various (largely organisational) factors on which the relative gestation lags will depend are likely to differ even more between countries and regions than the productivity of men and machines.

Chapter 4 discusses various problems of implementing labour-intensive techniques. It is shown that, in cases where there is a divergence between social and market profitability, public sector road construction methods should be based on shadow price calculations. If the projects are undertaken by the private sector, the differences between shadow and market prices give the taxes and subsidies which are required to make relative market prices correspond to relative social prices. As the shadow prices have been derived by explicitly taking account of any over-all fiscal (savings) constraint with which the country may be faced, *ex hypothesi* the implementation of projects which are socially profitable at these shadow prices cannot result in any additional fiscal problem.

In Chapter 4 we also describe the current bidding and administrative procedures as well as other institutional factors which lead to a capital-intensive bias in road construction techniques in the Philippines, even though (as our estimates in Chapters 2 and 3 show) many labour-intensive techniques are more profitable than equipment-intensive techniques at market prices. Finally, we discuss the important organisational problems involved in managing large bodies of men, and argue for the desirability of creating a more permanent labour force in the construction sector.

In conclusion, it should be stressed that, although this study successfully demonstrates the technical and economic efficiency of labour-intensive techniques for certain road construction tasks in the Philippines, this cannot be taken to be a blanket endorsement of any and every labour-intensive technique; nor will the techniques devised in this study necessarily be appropriate for other countries and climes. A detailed techno-economic case-by-case approach is essential. In this approach both shadow pricing of inputs and outputs and the derivation of reliable productivity estimates from field experiments will be required.

PRELIMINARY CONSIDERATIONS

1

This study is an empirical contribution to the current debate on the feasibility and social desirability of developing and using intermediate labour-intensive technologies in developing countries. As these debates are concerned with alleviating the employment problems of labour-surplus developing countries, the Philippines—with a recently estimated unemployment rate[1] (which includes both open unemployment and underemployment) of 25 per cent—is a suitable country for study.

The choice of the construction sector for our attempt to derive and evaluate an appropriate labour-intensive technology, however, requires some further justification. Moreover, it is also necessary to set our results in a wider perspective, as this will enable judgements about the feasibility and social desirability of adopting intermediate technologies in other sectors to be assessed. Again, as our views are to some extent at variance with received views, it is also necessary to outline briefly the general reasons for these differing conclusions. This preliminary chapter therefore attempts to place the study as a whole into this wider context.

TECHNOLOGY AND EMPLOYMENT

The employment problem has emerged as the most important and challenging current problem facing the Third World. Two major aspects of this problem have attracted the attention of most observers: resource utilisation, and income distribution or poverty. With regard to the first of these aspects, the employment problem is essentially a problem of the surplus of labour time available in developing countries which cannot be fully utilised without an increase in the supply of co-operant factors of production. The poverty aspect stresses the link between employment and incomes, and hence the relatively low level of incomes that the unemployed or underemployed are condemned to accept because of the lack of adequate high-productivity jobs, and/or the lack of any adequate transfer

---

[1] ILO: *Sharing in development . . .,* op. cit., p. 7.

mechanism for distributing a given aggregate income more equitably.[1] In this study we shall be concerned mainly with the resource utilisation aspect of the employment problem, but it is obvious that the distributional aspect is not thereby excluded; in fact, in Appendix C, where we derive the social cost of labour in the Philippines, we shall be much concerned with both the efficiency and the equity aspects of increasing employment.

Furthermore, we shall be specifically concerned with the relationship between technology and employment: for even with a given supply of the other co-operant factors of production, the over-all level of employment will in large part depend upon the available technological possibilities for combining different quantities of labour with these other factors. Thus if it is technologically feasible to substitute the abundant labour for the scarce co-operant factors (to be labelled as the portmanteau "capital"), more employment and output could be generated than if such substitution possibilities were scarce or absent.

It is one of the inescapable facts of life today that, whereas the appropriate technology for labour-surplus developing countries would be relatively labour-intensive, given their endowments of capital and labour, the actual technology they use is most often capital-intensive. This reflects both the dependence of developing countries on technology developed in advanced countries with an abundance of capital and a scarcity of labour, as well as the various distortions in the markets for labour and capital in developing countries which lead to an artificially high wage/capital-rental ratio and hence to the higher private profitability of the relatively more capital-intensive techniques.

This raises two questions, one technical, the other economic, about the feasibility and desirability of devising and adopting relatively more labour-intensive techniques in developing countries. The technical problem concerns the feasibility of finding *technically efficient* ways of substituting labour for capital in production, whilst the economic question is whether, given such technological alternatives, it is socially desirable to adopt more labour-intensive techniques. We shall deal with both these problems in turn.

The scope for substitution

The technical feasibility of substituting labour for capital must ultimately be an engineering problem. However, it is important to note that the labour-intensive technique which is developed must not be inferior to the capital-intensive technique, in the sense that it must not use both more labour and more capital (including working capital) to produce the same output. It has been argued[2] that many traditional techniques *are* inferior in this sense. They use both more capital

---

[1] There is also the growth aspect, but this can be looked upon as one of intergenerational distribution. I have discussed these aspects as well as the views of various writers on the employment problem at greater length elsewhere (see Deepak Lal: "Employment, income distribution and a poverty redressal index", in *World Development* (Oxford), Mar./Apr. 1973; and idem: "Poverty and unemployment: A question of policy", in *South Asian Review* (London), July 1972). See also A. K. Sen: *Employment, technology and development* (Oxford, Clarendon Press for the International Labour Office, 1975).

[2] See Richard S. Eckaus: "The factor proportions problem in underdeveloped areas", in *The American Economic Review* (Menasha, Wis.), May 1960; P. N. Dhar and H. F. Lydall: *The role of small enterprises in Indian economic development* (London, Asia Publishing House, 1961); A. K. Sen: *Choice of techniques* (Oxford, Blackwell, 3rd ed., 1968).

and more labour than the modern alternatives—so much so that some writers[1] have argued that there may, in fact, be little possibility for efficient substitution in the technology of modern manufacturing industry, and hence that for all practical purposes the appropriate technology for producing a given product can be taken to be one with fairly fixed coefficients. This leaves two possibilities for reducing the capital-intensive bias in technological choice in developing countries.

The first is to invent a technology which is appropriate to the factor endowments of developing countries. There are a number of proponents of an intermediate technology of this kind[2] which is based on the plausible notion that, in the past, technical progress has not led to the development of non-inferior labour-intensive techniques; this is because the research and development specific to particular techniques have been concentrated in labour-scarce countries, which are interested mainly in increasing the over-all productivity of relatively capital-intensive techniques. Hence it is argued that, even though existing labour-intensive technologies may be inferior to capital-intensive ones, it may pay to devote resources towards their improvement. Whilst this argument is attractive, in practice it does not provide a real basis for determining the likely social profitability of *inventing* new intermediate technologies.

This therefore leads to the second obvious remedy for the efficient reduction of the capital intensity of production in developing countries, namely through the adoption of a more appropriate choice of products to be produced domestically —for even if the ratio of labour to capital inputs is fixed for every product, these are nevertheless likely to differ between different industries. Thus the domestic production of relatively more labour-intensive products will tend to raise the over-all labour-to-capital ratios (and hence employment) of the economy as a whole. However, it is argued, in most developing countries this choice of labour-intensive production is hindered by all kinds of distortions in the workings of their markets for factors and commodities, such that the relative price of capital to labour is too high. On this view, reforms of the domestic relative price structure, and in particular of the relative price of capital to labour, so that they more closely reflect real scarcities in the economy, become the centre-piece of policies for raising employment and incomes. We return to this aspect later in this chapter.

A third approach, and the one adopted in the engineering sections of this book, is to ask whether it is possible to disentangle those aspects of the technology in particular industries where, in the past, capital has been substituted for labour in an "essential" way, from those aspects in which its substitution is not essential and was probably due purely to rises in the cost of labour relative to that of

---

[1] For instance Eckaus, op. cit.

[2] The main advocate of this idea is E. F. Schumacher, in his *Small is beautiful* (London, Blond & Briggs, 1973). For a contrary view, see Lal: "Poverty and unemployment . . .", op. cit. For a theoretical justification, see Anthony B. Atkinson and Joseph E. Stiglitz: "A new view of technological change", in *The Economic Journal* (London), Sep. 1969. They introduce the notion of localised technical progress, whereby historically the production function has not shifted smoothly outwards—only the capital-intensive sections have done so. Hence they reach the conclusion that it may be worth while to devote resources to research on shifting the labour-intensive sections of the production function outwards, so that labour-intensive techniques are no longer inferior; but, as they recognise, this depends upon the extent to which capital-intensive techniques currently dominate labour-intensive ones, on the resources required to improve them, and so forth.

capital. In the former case it will not be feasible to initiate a reverse movement without inventing a new technology, whereas in the latter case it may be relatively easy to make adaptations to existing technology and make it relatively labour-intensive without making it inferior. In Appendix A we discuss the considerations which are relevant when determining the "essentiality" of the historical substitution of capital for labour in contemporary technology. The upshot of this discussion is that a return to the older techniques based on traditional handicraft tools (suitably though simply modified) may provide technically efficient alternative labour-intensive technological choices in those industries where technical progress (stimulated by a rise in the relative cost of labour to capital) has been characterised by the introduction of machines which are simply a glorified, magnified and more complicated version of handicraft tools. The construction industry is obviously the most suitable candidate for such exploration. The modified labour-intensive techniques in road construction described in this book are essentially an example of such reverse substitution of labour for capital; but even in road construction it is important to distinguish those operations in which the machines play an essential part in production (for instance, in maintaining a particular quality of road surface which requires a degree of accuracy and dexterity to which men, with simpler tools, cannot attain) from those where these factors are not of great significance and where the substitution of machines for men can be due to historical changes in relative factor (labour-capital) costs.

The desirability of substitution

Technical feasibility is, however, not a sufficient criterion for adopting particular "non-inferior" labour-intensive techniques. As the extensive literature on investment criteria has emphasised,[1] maximising current employment could conflict with various other social objectives such as future employment and income growth, and hence it will be necessary to derive and use the appropriate accounting or shadow prices which take account of alternative social objectives and the relevant constraints of resources and technological possibilities. Moreover, as in most developing countries the domestic relative price system is distorted, these accounting prices will also have to take account of such distortions. They will then need to be used for a social cost–benefit analysis of the alternative techniques, since the market prices which (together with the productivities of alternative techniques) determine *market* profitability may not be a correct indicator of the social prices at which the *social* profitability and hence social desirability of the alternative techniques can be reached. Appendix C therefore derives a large number of the key shadow or accounting prices for the Philippines (the methodology and a summary of the estimates is given in Chapter 3), which are then applied to the alternative techniques for road construction devised by the

---

[1] See Sen: *Choice of techniques*, op. cit.; I. M. D. Little and J. A. Mirrlees: *Project appraisal and planning for developing countries* (London, Heinemann, 1974); UNIDO: *Guidelines for project evaluation*, Project formulation and evaluation series, No. 2 (New York, United Nations, 1972; Sales No.: E.72.II.B.11); Deepak Lal: "Disutility of effort, migration, and the shadow wage-rate", in *Oxford Economic Papers* (Oxford), Mar. 1973; idem: *Methods of project analysis: A review*, World Bank staff occasional papers, No. 16 (Baltimore and London, Johns Hopkins University Press, 1974).

ILO engineers and outlined in Chapters 2 and 3. The resulting social profitability of these alternatives is then estimated and discussed in Chapter 4.

Finally, even if particular labour-intensive techniques are technically feasible and their adoption is socially desirable, it may nevertheless not be privately profitable to adopt such techniques at the existing market wage and capital-rental rates. There will then also be a problem of implementation, that is of devising the appropriate means of ensuring that the socially optimal techniques are in fact adopted. Chapter 4 deals with these and other implementation problems.

THE PROJECT

The project described in this study was aimed at developing and evaluating what are here called "modified" labour-intensive techniques for various tasks in road construction. The project was in two phases. In the first, which was conducted in conjunction with the ILO comprehensive employment strategy mission to the Philippines in June 1973, two ILO engineers devised a labour-intensive technology, based on suitable modifications of farm equipment traditionally used in the Philippines, for the construction of a pilot gravel road—the Capas–Botolan road.

This road follows the line of an ancient trail crossing the Zambales mountain range (see frontispiece and figure 1, which gives the typical road section). It will provide a short route between Central Zambales on the South China Sea coast and the Tarlac area of Central Luzon. Proposals for transforming the trail into a national highway were originally put forward in the time of President Quezon; location surveys were made in 1957, and some construction was subsequently carried out. The stretch still to be constructed between O'Donnell Barrio in Tarlac and Malumboy in Zambales is about 59 km in length. From Malumboy to Maquisquis in Zambales there is a logging road which serves several new sugar plantations and is passable in the dry season only, because of the need to ford several rivers or creeks. In places the line of the logging road is adjacent to the proposed line of the new construction. The unconstructed section between O'Donnell Barrio and Maquisquis is about 43 km long.

The road had been designated as a pilot research project by the Government of the Philippines, in order to experiment with alternative technologies for road construction and in particular to test the practical viability of labour-intensive methods of road construction. In the second phase of the project, therefore, the ILO engineers were directly involved in building parts of the Capas–Botolan road with their modified labour-intensive techniques and in comparing their results with those achieved through the conventional capital-intensive methods adopted previously. This meant that we had the unusually good fortune of being able to conduct that rarity in the social sciences, a virtual controlled experiment, to test the technical and economic viability of labour-intensive techniques in road construction in the Philippines.

In order to test the economic viability it was necessary to arrive at estimates of a wide range of shadow or accounting prices for various goods and services in the Philippine economy—a task that was completed during July–August 1973, partly in conjunction with the ILO comprehensive employment strategy mission. The engineering estimates of the expected relative productivity of men and

Figure 1. Typical roadway sections

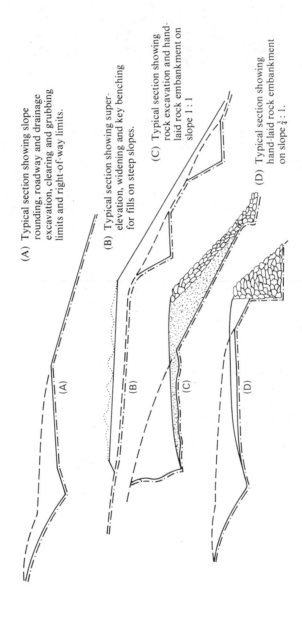

(A) Typical section showing slope rounding, roadway and drainage excavation, clearing and grubbing limits and right-of-way limits.

(B) Typical section showing super-elevation, widening and key benching for fills on steep slopes.

(C) Typical section showing rock excavation and hand-laid rock embankment on slope 1 : 1

(D) Typical section showing hand-laid rock embankment on slope $\frac{3}{4}$: 1.

machines on alternative road construction techniques arrived at by the ILO engineers during Phase I (referred to as *ex ante* estimates in this book), together with the shadow price estimates, were used to determine the relative social profitability of the alternative techniques, and as noted in the ILO mission report[1] they showed that labour-intensive techniques were more profitable than capital-intensive ones, at both market and shadow prices.

As a result of problems encountered in securing right of way, work on the road was not started until 17 January 1974. By May the first two kilometres were virtually complete and work on the next three kilometres was well advanced. The road will ultimately have a 6·10 m asphalt concrete pavement with 1·5 m shoulders on both sides. At first it will be surfaced with gravel; an asphalt carpet is to be laid three or four years later.

As reported in detail in the appendices to this book, the ILO engineers concluded from their field experiments that their *ex ante* estimates of the productivity of men and machines were fairly close to reality, and hence our earlier conclusions about the technical and economic viability of labour-intensive road construction techniques in the Philippines were quite justified.

---

[1] ILO: *Sharing in development* . . ., op. cit., Ch. 6.

TECHNIQUES AND PRODUCTIVITIES

2

The report of the ILO comprehensive employment strategy mission to the Philippines summarised the salient features of the country's public infrastructure programme.[1] Most government expenditure has been devoted to highways and bridges, with a heavy regional concentration. The 1974–77 Development Plan gives top priority to infrastructure development, which it recognises has been inadequate in the past.

The report gives the following estimates of the national stock of roads in June 1972: expressways, 47 km; primary and secondary roads, 49,418 km; and feeder roads, 32,123 km. This gives a total of 81,588 km. Of these roads, 80 per cent were earth or gravel, 15 per cent were paved with asphalt, and about 5 per cent were paved with concrete. The 1974–77 highways programme calls for the rehabilitation of 2,326 km of concrete-paved roads, 2,212 km of asphalt-paved roads, and 20,510 km of gravel roads.

There is a growing interest in the Philippines in adopting labour-intensive methods in the infrastructure programme. One of the declared objectives of the 1974–77 Development Plan was the extensive application of labour-intensive methods in infrastructure development. In October 1972 the Department of Public Works, Transportation and Communication set up a committee to study labour-intensive construction methods,[2] and it also successfully supported a pilot project on labour-intensive methods on levee construction. Subsequently, a draft manual for the construction of flood control levees by labour-intensive methods was prepared and the committee advocated its adoption.

In August 1973 the Bureau of Public Highways[3] issued guidelines on the construction of feeder (farm to market) roads. These guidelines included a paragraph requiring that "in support of government policies for reducing unemployment by way of adopting labour-intensive techniques, the engineer should as far as possible give preference to the use of labour rather than mechanical equipment. Side hill grading and other road works involving light earthmoving and grading should, as much as possible, be done by rural labourers employing the . . .

---

[1] See ILO: *Sharing in development . . .*, op. cit., Ch. 6.

[2] The Department of Public Highways is also intending to set up such a committee.

[3] By Presidential Decree of 16 May 1974 the Bureau was transformed into the Department of Public Highways. This new arrangement is intended to speed up the highways programme.

packquiao system.[1] Mechanisation should be limited to long hauls or heavy earthworks or to sparsely populated areas only, where labour shortages exist."

In view of this directive and of the previous work on levee construction, the Department of Public Works, Transportation and Communication proposed that the construction of the Capas–Botolan road be used as a pilot project to assess the feasibility of using labour-intensive methods in gravel road construction. As we have seen, this pilot project has indicated the technical feasibility of constructing roads by labour-intensive methods, even under the severe conditions obtaining on this site: the terrain ranges from flat to mountainous, and the soil types encountered ranged from alluvial sand, gravel and sandy loam to hard clay and soft rock. Cut and fill was sometimes up to 6 m deep. A considerable amount of data was accumulated through field studies on different working methods appropriate to the various site conditions, and on the best composition of the various work teams, their output and their unit costs. A general description of the various methods used is given below, and technical data are presented in Appendix B.

It was not possible to study some operations since the appropriate equipment could not be obtained. These were chiefly the compaction of fill by vibrating-plate compactor and the haulage of fill material by tractor/trailer combination. Data on these operations are vital to the successful implementation of labour-intensive road construction. Where they occur in the case study, output and cost data from other sources have been used.

LABOUR-INTENSIVE TECHNIQUES USED

Carabao[2]-drawn plough (plate 1)

The plough, as normally used in the rice-fields, was used for:
(a) grubbing and clearing—to loosen topsoil so as to facilitate the removal of roots and vegetable matter; and
(b) excavation—to loosen the earth so as to facilitate subsequent digging and loading by either hand-tools or carabao-drawn scraper.

Further experiments are required to devise a similar implement which is more effective for carrying out this type of work in very hard ground.

Carabao-drawn scraper (plate 2)

Traditional

The scraper is made by basket-weaving split bamboo through the tynes or prongs of the harrow normally used in the rice-fields. Approximately ten pieces of split bamboo about 1 m long are required, the cost being negligible since bamboo is generally available around the *barrio*.[3] Labour in cutting, splitting and fixing is about 0·5 man-hour. The scrapers can be used for:

---

[1] *Packquiao* system: see Appendix B, p. 63, fn. 1.

[2] Water buffalo.

[3] A *barrio* is a group of dwellings. It may constitute a hamlet, a village, a suburb or an urban district.

Plate 1.   Carabao-drawn plough

(*a*) clearing and grubbing (using the harrow without the split bamboo for combing out the roots);

(*b*) excavating and transporting previously loosened earth over short distances; and

(*c*) grading and spreading fill materials.

Oil-drum scraper (plate 3)

This type was made on site by cutting a section from a 44-gallon drum, and welding suitable attachments to it so that it could be towed by a carabao. It is used exclusively for excavating and transporting earth over short distances. It can be improved.[1]

Factory-made scraper (plate 4)

This type was designed some years ago for use on a progressive hacienda, and was introduced on the initiative of Secretary David M. Consunji of the Department of Public Works, Transportation and Communication. It was made in a Manila factory. The first version was subsequently modified to give improved handling. One dozen of the modified version were manufactured at a cost of 750

[1] Similar types are described in Volunteers for International Technical Assistance (VITA): *Village technology handbook* (Schenectady, NY, 1970), section on "Earth-moving devices for irrigation and road-building". This volume is a revised version of the earlier USAID handbook of the same name, now out of print.

Plate 2.   Carabao-drawn scraper

Plate 3.   Oil-drum scraper

pesos each (= approx. US$110). This type of carabao-drawn scraper was used exclusively for the excavation and transportation of loosened earth over short distances, including side cut and fill, and was the most productive of the three types.

These factory-made scrapers are capable of further minor improvement, and larger-scale production would reduce their cost again. They are extremely

Plate 4.   Factory-made scraper

Plate 5. Modified carabao-drawn cart. The bamboo mat has a handle for withdrawing it from the cart, thus allowing the earth to fall out of the bottom

Plate 6. Modified carabao-drawn cart, using long bamboo mats. With this type two men are needed to discharge the earth

Plate 7.   Modified carabao-drawn cart

Plate 8.   Carabao-drawn cart in use

Plate 9.   Wooden-wheeled cart with two carabao

Plate 10.   Carabao-drawn cart with rubber-tyred wheels, in soft sand

robust; they have however not been in use long enough to show signs of wear, so that it has been necessary to estimate their working life (which could possibly be extended by the incorporation of replaceable runners and cutting edges).

Carabao-drawn carts (plates 5–10)

The carabao-drawn cart was used for the haulage of fill and road base material, and output and cost data were prepared for haulage distances of up to 1 km. The carts were modified, at an approximate cost of 20 pesos (about US$3·00), to carry excavated material up to a capacity of 0·3 m³ struck level and to be bottom-emptying. Plates 5 to 10 indicate the method of construction and use.

Rubber-tyred carts are preferred because they require less tractive effort and give better compaction than steel-rimmed wooden wheels. A second-hand cart will cost 500 to 750 pesos (US$75 to $110) depending on condition, and conversion from wooden wheels to (second-hand) rubber-tyred wheels will cost about 250 pesos. However, some farmers are reluctant to carry out this conversion because of the problem of repairing flat tyres.

Further research is required to improve the method; for instance, the time for emptying the carts varied from as little as ten seconds for dry, cohesion-less river sand to over two minutes when clay materials were transported. This latter time could be reduced.

Wheelbarrows (plate 11)

In general, wheelbarrows proved to be the most expensive method of transportation. Under the strategy used on the labour-intensive case study this method was used only on terrain inaccessible to other types of transportation—but only until the excavation had advanced sufficiently to permit the introduction of more economical methods.

The type of wheelbarrow produced by the Bureau of Public Highways was the cheapest available. It had steel wheels and the balance was not optimal for good handling. These barrows were suitable for work on firm ground, but the tractive effort required increased on soft ground. The productivity figures for this type have been used in the study; however, it is considered that a robust, rubber-tyred wheelbarrow, though initially more expensive, would prove to be cheaper in use.

Watering by carabao-drawn water cart

An analysis was made of this method of watering fill material prior to compaction. Two types of tank have been manufactured and found satisfactory in use: the drum type and the rectangular type. Both types can be mounted on an ordinary bull-cart frame and are filled by hand using a water bucket. Baffles are needed in the rectangular tank in order to restrict the internal movement of water. The two types are shown in plates 12 and 13.

Plate 11.   Transporting soil by wheelbarrow

Plate 12.   Water tank (drum type)

Plate 13.   Water tank (rectangular type)

Only the drum type was used on the project. The costs of manufacture (1972 prices) were: drum type, 200 pesos (US$30·00); rectangular type, 300 pesos (US$53·00).[1]

Tractor/trailer combinations

In this method one tractor is used with several trailers for transporting fill material. Thus, instead of a whole dump-truck unit standing idle whilst it is being hand loaded, only the trailer is stationary: the tractor, which is the expensive component of the combination, is fully occupied in shuttling trailers back and forth. It is considered that this mode of transportation may be economically competitive with dump-truck/payloader combinations for distances up to 10 km, subject to site conditions. The *ex ante* estimates for this type of work were based on the ILO engineers' estimates, and it was hoped that the Capas–Botolan project would provide opportunities for practical study. However, as stated earlier, it was not possible to procure such equipment. Consequently the revised estimates were made on the same judgements as the *ex ante* estimates of 1973, but were supplemented by appropriate productivity data which were collected subsequently in the Philippines.

---

[1] Cost data from Department of Public Works, Transportation and Communication: *Construction of levees by labour-intensive methods* (Manila, 1972).

Hand excavation

This activity was studied for various tasks, from ditching to the loading of carts, in various types of soil from soft sand to soft rock. Since many labourers were required to provide their own hand-tools, their quality was not of the best. Productivity could be raised by the provision of better hand-tools.

Dump-truck/payloader combinations

The *ex ante* estimates used for this method of loading and hauling base material were based on locally available data. The revised estimates have been adopted in the light of subsequent studies made in the Philippines.

Compaction

As stated above, excavation and filling were carried out in some localities that were accessible only to wheelbarrows. Consequently, not only was it impossible for conventional rollers to gain access, but even if they had been able to do so, they would have been grossly under-utilised because of the relatively low rate of excavation and fill by hand labour and wheelbarrow. It was therefore proposed that both these problems be solved by using one-man, hand-operated vibrating-plate compactors. In the event, it was not possible to obtain such a compactor so that their performance could not be evaluated. However, compactors of this type are manufactured locally, and their use has been assumed and their daily cost and productivity has been estimated for the study.

PRODUCTIVITY

In this section we outline the various assessments of productivity made for alternative techniques during the study.

Estimates were initially made in June–July 1973, prior to the construction of the road. In making these *ex ante* estimates of the productivity of labour and equipment, both available data and informed judgements were used.

Subsequently, during the actual construction stage, the productivity of these alternatives was evaluated by on-site studies. The validity of the original *ex ante* estimates was thus tested, and it was, moreover, possible to make improvements in the design of what we have called modified labour-intensive techniques.

Thus we have, first, the original *ex ante* productivity estimates; and second, the actual productivity of alternative techniques derived from the field studies on the Capas–Botolan road (these latter estimates being referred to in this study as revised estimates). The results are also used to arrive at productivity estimates for alternative techniques for building an average gravel road in the Philippines. Finally, as the principles on which the labour-intensive techniques have been devised can be extended to the design of alternative techniques for various road construction activities not undertaken on the Capas–Botolan project, estimates were also made of the productivity of alternative techniques for paving roads with concrete and for the excavation and hauling of fill materials.

Alternative estimates for the Capas–Botolan experiment

In June 1973 the Bureau of Public Highways prepared two estimates for constructing the Capas–Botolan road; one for labour-intensive methods, the other for capital-intensive ones. These were examined by two of the ILO engineers, and certain modifications were made in consultation with departmental representatives (for example, in rental rates for commercial equipment). The engineers also prepared a third estimate—the modified labour-intensive method—which eliminated the use of some labour-intensive methods considered to be of doubtful feasibility and introduced the use of tractor/trailer combinations for hauling materials by the labour-intensive methods.

The resulting *ex ante* and revised productivity estimates are summarised in Appendix B, where full details of the method of calculation are given.

Estimates for an average gravel road

The Capas–Botolan road is, however, not likely to be a typical Philippine road. The ILO engineers, in consultation with engineers from the Bureau of Public Highways, therefore derived estimates for an average gravel road in the Philippines. The main assumption is that the earthworks and some of the other items on the Capas–Botolan road were twice the national average. The Capas–Botolan estimates were then suitably adjusted to derive the data for the construction of an average gravel road with the same cross-section as the Capas–Botolan road. These estimates are obviously crucially dependent on the above assumption. They were derived for the capital-intensive and modified labour-intensive alternatives.

Alternative techniques for concrete paving of roads

Attempts were also made to design labour-intensive techniques for other tasks in road construction which were not represented on the Capas–Botolan gravel road. One of these was for the concrete paving of roads. Hand-placing methods to replace concrete-paving machines were devised which could, subject to adequate engineering supervision, result in concrete paving of equivalent quality. Data for the two alternatives were obtained from two actual projects in the Philippines and are given in Appendix B.

Excavation and hauling of fill material

Another obvious area where the substitution of men for machines would appear to be feasible is in the excavation and haulage tasks involved in road construction. Estimates based upon various sources (chiefly local, except for the tractor/trailer combination) were prepared for alternative methods of excavating and hauling fill material over various haulage distances up to 10 km. These estimates were then revised in the light of the field experiment results from the Capas–Botolan road. As there was not much difference between the *ex ante* and revised estimates, only the latter are detailed in Appendix B.

The basis of the labour-intensive alternative was the use of farm tractors and trailers. Apart from the versatility of the farm tractor, the advantage of tractor/trailer combinations is, as we have seen, that the expensive component of the combination (the tractor) is kept fully employed, and only the trailer[1] is subject to standing time when it is hand-loaded (two or more trailers being hand-loaded, depending on the haulage distance). In the alternative technology, in the case of dump-trucks, it is necessary to load by machine to cut down expensive standing time.

Fortunately, as a result of the field experiments conducted on the Capas–Botolan road during the second phase of this study, we were able to test the accuracy of the *ex ante* productivity estimates. It should be noted that, as the purely labour-intensive method was not implemented, no revised estimates on the basis of field observations appear for this alternative. For the others (capital-intensive and modified labour-intensive methods) it appears that the *ex ante* labour productivity rates were equalled or surpassed in practice on the Capas–Botolan road.

There were some changes in productivity rates in the revised estimates as compared with the *ex ante* estimates, as can be seen from Appendix B; however, given the general level of reliability of any engineering data, the range of variation lies well within the "acceptable" margin.

In Chapter 3 we evaluate the economic desirability of alternative techniques on both the *ex ante* and the revised estimates of productivities.

---

[1] It should also be noted that local industry is fully competent to manufacture trailers.

PRICES

3

In Chapter 2 we saw from field experiments in the Philippines that intermediate labour-intensive techniques *can* be devised and that these are not inferior to capital-intensive techniques of road construction. However, if we are to assess whether the adoption of these intermediate technologies is socially desirable, we must assess the relative social profitability of the alternative techniques. For this we need to know not only the productivity of men and machines under the alternative techniques detailed in Appendix B but also the *social* prices at which the alternative inputs of the various techniques are to be evaluated.

The general framework for assessing social profitability will be the same accounting framework within which, say, a private contractor will assess the private profitability of alternative techniques by evaluating, in terms of some common yardstick, the various quantities of goods and services making up the costs of the alternative techniques. For the private contractor the yardstick is the money cost of each of the techniques, with the various quantities of the goods and services used being valued at their market prices, and he will choose the technique with the lowest money costs. This would also be the procedure a public authority should follow—if the relative market prices of all the goods and services used accurately reflected the relative social costs of using these goods and services. However, for a number of reasons outlined below, in most developing countries market prices will not reflect social values; it will therefore be necessary to determine shadow or accounting prices, which must then be used to weight the quantities of goods and services used by different techniques to determine their relative social profitability.

The second section of this chapter therefore outlines the methodology used to arrive at a comprehensive set of shadow prices for the Philippines. Fuller details are given in Appendix C. It may be noted that this is the first comprehensive set of shadow prices to be estimated for the Philippines, and that the prices should be used in appraising a wide variety of economic policies, even though in this book we shall be using only some of them. For our purpose we require estimates of the shadow prices of equipment and labour. Again, fuller details are given in Appendix C; however, in the third section of this chapter we summarise the estimates we have arrived at for the social evaluation of the alternative techniques to be discussed in Chapter 4.

THE NEED FOR ACCOUNTING (SHADOW) PRICES

The principle underlying all methods of measuring social costs and benefits is that they should reflect the impact on social welfare of using or producing various inputs and outputs. This involves two types of weighting problems which cannot be solved by merely applying market prices. Any investment project is a method of changing the time profile of consumption: that is, it involves giving up consumption (saving and investment) at certain dates in order to obtain consumption flows at later dates. Thus investment provides a flow of consumption in the future, and alternative investments will provide different time profiles of consumption flows. From a social viewpoint, a government's over-all objective in investment planning can then be taken to be the choice of a time profile of aggregate consumption which maximises the sum of the social value of consumption accruing at different dates. This involves consumption changes for different generations. To make these commensurable, we need to assign distributional weights for the relative welfare of different generations, in order to obtain the social values attached to dated consumption. This problem of weighting costs or gains accruing to different generations is the same as that of determining suitable rates of interest to be used in discounting future costs and benefits. It cannot be solved by merely looking at market rates of interest, because (apart from the problem of assigning any social value to these rates) they vary enormously with the market under consideration.

When a private individual is saving and investing, he too is making decisions about his own intertemporal consumption profile, but when making these choices he is likely to be moved only by his own relative welfare during his lifetime. However, as society—at least in principle—is immortal (unlike individuals), it has to take account of the relative welfare of *all* future generations. Other things being equal, therefore, the savings (future consumption) generated as a result of the decisions of private savers are likely to be less than socially optimal. Hence a government may, as the custodian of the welfare of all generations, want to raise the level of savings in the economy above that desired by private individuals. To express this divergence between private and social goals it is sometimes said that the rate at which society discounts future consumption (and hence the welfare of future generations) is lower than that used by private individuals.

Furthermore, society also has to assign relative social weights to the changes in consumption of different income groups within generations, which are induced by its investment decisions. In both the inter- and the intratemporal dimensions the gain of consumption of a "rich" generation/person will be less highly valued than that of a "poor" one. These weighting problems involve essential social value judgements. The national plan provides these basic judgements to the project appraiser, and they must be accepted and incorporated in deriving the relevant weights.

Finally, market prices may also fail to provide suitable weights for the social valuation of quantities of inputs or outputs because of distortions in product and factor markets. Under a perfectly functioning price mechanism, market prices of goods and factors are equal to the marginal social cost (MSC) of production and the marginal social value (MSV) of using the relevant goods and factors. Distortions, however, drive a wedge between the MSC and MSV for goods and factors. These divergences between MSC and MSV can be caused by taxes, monopolies, externalities, increasing returns, and so on. One of the most important sources of distortion in the relative prices in many developing countries is the foreign trade control system used to manage the balance of payments and to provide protection to domestic industries. This often tends to lead to widely varying rates of protection for different goods or activities.

For all these reasons, relative market prices will not give a correct indication of the relative social values of different goods and services in the economy. We shall now describe the principles on which we propose to derive the social prices to be used for valuing the inputs and outputs of investment projects.

METHODOLOGY OF ESTIMATING ACCOUNTING PRICES

We shall adopt the methodology followed in the volume by I. M. D. Little and J. A. Mirrlees[1] to derive shadow or accounting prices for the Philippines.

In deriving accounting prices we need some unit of account or numeraire, to make commensurable the different costs and benefits of an investment project. Little and Mirrlees take uncommitted government income expressed in foreign exchange as their numeraire; we shall adopt a slightly altered version of this, namely aggregate savings in terms of foreign exchange.[2] This may appear odd, because economists normally regard consumption expressed in the local currency as the source of economic welfare.[3] However, it should be noted that the costs and benefits of an investment project can be broken down into (a) local currency and foreign currency items; and (b) benefits and costs which accrue at different points in time, and hence represent consumption forgone or gained at different dates. Thus the general problem is to make commensurable what might loosely be called four "commodities", namely local currency, foreign currency, and present and future consumption. As long as the same set of weights (relative prices) is used to make these four commodities commensurable, it is purely a matter of convenience whether we take as our numeraire present consumption expressed in terms of local currency or future consumption (which depends on current savings) expressed in foreign exchange.[4] Our adoption of the latter, therefore, still expresses the net benefits of investment projects in terms of their effects on social aggregate welfare.

The basic thesis of Little and Mirrless is that, in relatively open economies where the market price structure has been distorted by the imposition of differentiated protective structures, relative social values of commodities are better measured in terms of relative "border" prices—that is, the prices the country has to pay for its imports or obtains for its exports of the relevant commodities (assuming that it cannot influence its terms of trade, in which case the relevant marginal costs/revenues in foreign trade of the commodities will be

---

[1] I. M. D. Little and J. A. Mirrlees: *Social cost benefit analysis*, Vol. II of OECD: *Manual of industrial project analysis in developing countries* (Paris, 1969). A revised edition has been published.

[2] This implies that unlike Little and Mirrlees we shall not differentiate the social value of the "savings" of different groups.

[3] This in fact is the numeraire adopted in UNIDO: *Guidelines for project evaluation*, op. cit.

[4] The formal equivalence of the Little–Mirrlees and UNIDO methods is shown in Lal: *Methods of project analysis: A review*, op. cit., which also gives reasons why in practice the methods of Little and Mirrlees may be more convenient to use than those of UNIDO.

their accounting prices). These border prices will be the relevant accounting prices for fully traded goods, i.e. for goods for which the impact of marginal changes in domestic demand and supply, directly or indirectly, can be taken to be on foreign trade. For goods which do not enter foreign trade at all because of prohibitive transport costs, the accounting prices will be given by the cost of producing these non-traded goods in terms of our numeraire, with savings expressed in terms of foreign exchange. This is the method Little and Mirrlees adopt for valuing non-traded goods, whose increased demand is met by increased production. There will, however, be a third category of goods, which can be labelled "partially traded", for which the impact of an increase in demand could be on domestic production, foreign trade and domestic consumption. It will be necessary to determine the proportions in which the extra demand is met from each of the above three sources. Given this, the social costs of meeting the demand will just be the weighted average of the social costs of a marginal increase in domestic production, decrease in domestic consumption and increase (decrease) in imports (exports) of the goods. The weights are the estimates of the proportionate share of these alternative sources in meeting the increase in demand. For the proportions which come from foreign trade and domestic production, the above general principles for determining social costs can be used. As regards the proportion which comes from decreased consumption, the effect of the increased demand for the partially traded good would have led to some bidding up of its domestic price, and hence the switching of consumer expenditure away from it to other goods and services. The accounting cost of providing these alternative goods and services to consumers will then be the social cost of obtaining the goods from domestic consumption for use on the project. It will normally not be possible to determine the "other goods and services" to which consumers shift their expenditure. Moreover, if we assume that they consist of the same goods and services which make up the average consumption bundle for the economy, by revaluing the components of this bundle at accounting prices we can determine its total accounting value. The ratio of the value of the consumption bundle at market prices to that at accounting prices will be the average *aggregate consumption conversion factor*[1] for the economy. If the particular groups whose consumption is affected by the increase in project demand for a particular goods item can be identified, then (given their expenditure pattern) specific consumption conversion factors can be derived for any particular group of consumers.

This takes account of the general principles on which the social costs and benefits of "produced" inputs and outputs can be computed.

Next let us consider the valuation of primary factors: labour, land and capital. Given the distortions in factor markets, again relative market prices for these factors will not give a good estimate of their relative social values.

For labour, it will be necessary to determine the accounting prices of different types of labour which are distinct from each other as regards both quality and their location in space and time. Thus the accounting price of seasonally unemployed agricultural labour will be different from that of skilled urban labour

---

[1] This corresponds to the shadow exchange rate (SER) used on certain project appraisal methods, e.g. UNIDO: *Guidelines for project evaluation*, op. cit. For a comparison of the relative desirability of a single SER and multiple conversion factors along OECD lines, see Deepak Lal: "Adjustments for trade distortions in project analysis", in *The Journal of Development Studies* (London), Oct. 1974.

employed in modern factories. In determining the accounting prices of a parti-cular class of labour, in general two main sets of considerations will have to be taken into account. The first is the output forgone in its earlier employment valued in terms of foreign exchange (our numeraire) resulting from the employment of a labourer on the investment project being appraised. The second is to weight any income gains which the worker or his family might receive if the wage paid in his new employment is greater than the wage he received in his previous employ-ment. These weights will have to reflect various social objectives such as the desired change in both the intra- and the intertemporal distribution of income and consumption. They must ultimately depend upon value judgements; but there are obvious advantages in deriving them from an explicit and consistent set of such judgements. Given these weights, the net social cost of the increase in the workers' consumption in terms of our numeraire (savings expressed in foreign exchange) can be determined and added to the social cost of the output forgone by his employment on the project to yield the accounting wage.

For land it will be necessary to estimate the value marginal product of land of differing quality and location, in an alternative use, again in terms of our numeraire.

This leaves capital, both fixed and working. For fixed capital we require estimates of the accounting value of each particular capital good at replacement cost. Working capital is valued by costing each of its components at accounting prices.

Having applied the above rules, we are left with a stream of net project benefits at accounting prices. This stream has to be reduced to a single figure: the net social present value (NSPV) of the project. The investment criterion is that one should accept any project for which the NSPV is positive. To obtain the present value of the stream of net project benefits we need a discount rate. The appropriate discount rate with savings as the numeraire is the accounting rate of interest (ARI).[1] This is defined as the social rate of return to investment valued in terms of savings. Given the ARI, we have all the components for conducting social cost–benefit analysis.

ACCOUNTING PRICES FOR THE PHILIPPINES

Part A of table 1 summarises the accounting ratios for various commodities that we have determined in Appendix C. *These accounting ratios are the ratios of the market price of the goods to their accounting price.* Accounting ratios are given in this table for a large number of tradeable goods and the major non-traded goods in the economy. The former were required to estimate the latter: hence in cases where the border prices of traded goods are not directly known, the accounting ratios for the particular traded goods could be used from table 1 to determine the accounting value (price). This will be given by dividing the value (price) at market prices by the relevant accounting ratio.

It will be seen from table 1 that accounting ratios are given for producer prices (A^p) and for consumer prices (A^c). The difference between them is largely accounted for by trade margins and indirect taxes. Given the market value of these two items, the accounting cost of trade margins is added to the accounting producer price of the commodity to determine its accounting consumer price.

---

[1] See Little and Mirrlees: *Social cost benefit analysis*, op. cit.

Table 1.   Summary of accounting prices for the Philippines

A. Accounting ratios for commodities $\left(A = \dfrac{P^m}{P^a} \right)$

Code number. 33-sector breakdown	Code number. 194-sector breakdown	Sector	Producer price (A^p)	Consumer price (A^c)
I. Traded goods				
17		*Modern consumer goods*	*1·18*	*1·52*
	035	Processed meat products	1·73	1·64
	039	Preserved vegetables and other preserved fruits	1·56	1·53
	046	Cocoa, chocolate and sugar confectioneries	1·41	1·39
	047	Processed coffee	1·41	1·39
	051	Starch and starch products	1·94	1·79
	053	Other food preparations	1·12	1·15
	054	Distilled and blended spirits and brewery products	1·17	1·35
	056	Soft drinks	1·12	1·31
	057	Cigars and cigarettes	1·20	1·65
	059	Textile mill products	1·32	1·33
	060	Knitting mill products	1·12	1·17
	066	Embroidery products	1·13	1·16
	067	Other made-up textile goods	1·13	1·16
	073	Wood and rattan furniture and fixtures	1·11	1·18
	079	Other paper products	1·73	1·64
	085	Leather products	1·08	1·13
	086	Rubber footwear and garments	1·12	1·16
	093	Medical and pharmaceutical preparations	1·27	1·27
	094	Soap and other washing compounds	1·15	1·18
	095	Cosmetic and toilet preparations	1·98	1·78
	097	Matches	1·27	1·27
	118	Household-type appliances	1·80	1·65
	121	Electrical communication equipment	2·50	2·12
	124	Household electrical appliances	1·92	1·76
18		*Traditional consumer goods*	*1·17*	*1·20*
	036	Ice-cream products	1·68	1·61
	041	Milled rice	1·17	1·19
	042	Milled maize	1·17	1·19
	044	Bakery products	1·17	1·19
	055	Wines	1·17	1·35
	062	Other textile products	1·32	1·33
	063	Footwear	1·08	1·13
	064	Ready-made clothing	1·12	1·16
	110	Cutlery, hand-tools and general hardware	1·47	1·46
	125	Other electrical apparatus, equipment and appliances	2·28	2·00
	130	Bicycles and motorcycles	1·33	1·34
	131	Other transport equipment	1·56	1·54
	132	Photographic, optical and ophthalmic goods	2·00	1·87
	133	Jewellery, silverware and plated ware	3·55	2·78
	134	Musical instruments	2·82	2·40
	135	Fabricated plastic products	1·76	1·69

Code number, 33-sector breakdown	Code number, 194-sector breakdown	Sector	Producer price (A^p)	Consumer price (A^c)
19		*Modern intermediate goods*	*1·18*	*1·28*
	043	Flour and other grain mill products	1·17	1·19
	050	Animal feeds	1·07	1·10
	061	Cordage, twine and net	0·93	1·00
	068	Sawmill and planing mill products	0·93	1·00
	070	Mill work products	1·16	1·20
	071	Wooden containers	1·24	1·26
	076	Pulp, paper, paperboard	1·33	1·33
	077	Paper products	1·10	1·14
	078	Paperboard products	1·10	1·14
	082	Commercial printing	1·31	1·34
	084	Tanned or finished leather	2·08	1·87
	087	Tyres and inner tubes	1·53	1·52
	089	Other rubber products	1·11	1·16
	090	Basic industrial chemicals	1·20	1·21
	092	Paints, varnishes and related compounds	1·12	1·16
	096	Fertiliser	1·18	1·20
	098	Other chemical products	1·26	1·26
	099	Products of petroleum and coal	1·14	1·40
	100	Hydraulic cement	1·26	1·29
	101	Structural concrete products	1·08	1·13
	102	Structural clay products	1·20	1·24
	103	Glass and glass products	1·47	1·46
	106	Blast and electric furnace and rolling mill products	1·31	1·33
	107	Iron and steel foundry products	1·11	1·16
	111	Fabricated structural metal products	1·83	1·76
	113	Fabricated wire products	1·30	1·32
	115	Other fabricated metal products	1·42	1·42
	123	Electric lamps and bulbs	2·28	2·00
	128	Motor vehicle parts and supplies	1·20	1·22
20		*Modern capital goods*	*1·25*	*1·27*
	074	Metal furniture and fixtures	2·06	1·96
	075	Other furniture and fixtures	0·93	1·01
	112	Stamped, coated and engraved metals	1·14	1·17
	116	Tractors and farm machinery	1·16	1·19
	117	Industrial machinery	1·16	1·19
	119	Other machinery, except electrical	1·42	1·39
	120	Electrical industrial apparatus	1·27	1·24
	122	Batteries	1·52	1·48
	127	Motor vehicles	1·31	1·37
21		*Export-oriented manufactured goods*	*1·05*	*1·10*
	038	Canned fruits and fruit juices	0·93	0·99
	045	Milled and refined sugar	1·37	1·36
	048	Dessicated coconut products	0·93	0·99
	069	Plywood and veneer	0·93	0·99
	091	Vegetable and animal oils and fats	1·09	1·17

Table 1. (*contd.*)

A. Accounting ratios for commodities (*contd.*)

Code number, 33-sector breakdown	Code number, 194-sector breakdown	Sector	Producer price (A^p)	Consumer price (A^c)
		II. Non-traded goods		
22		*Construction*	*1·38*	
23		*Public utilities*	*1·68*	*1·39*
24		*Wholesale trade*	*1·23*	
25		*Retail trade*	*1·23*	
26		*Finance*	*1·23*	
27		*Rents*	*1·52*	*1·59*
28		*Modern transportation and communications*	*1·87*	*1·88*
29		*Traditional transportation*	*1·996*	
30		*Government*	*1·25*	
31		*Modern services*	*1·60*	*1·60*
32		*Traditional services*	*1·16*	*1·18*

B. Consumption conversion factors ($C = C^M - C^A$)

Region or household income group	C
I (Manila)	1·29
II (Ilocos)	1·36
III (Cagayan Valley)	1·17
IV (Central Luzon)	1·36
V (Southern Tagalog)	1·22
VI (Bicol)	1·19
VII (Western Visayas)	1·21
VIII (Eastern Visayas)	1·21
IX (Northern and Eastern Mindanao)	1·19
X (Southern and Western Mindanao)	1·16
All Philippines	*1·23*
Urban household income group	*1·25*
3 000–3 999 pesos	1·23
4 000–4 999 ,,	1·24
8 000–9 999 ,,	1·26
10 000–14 999 ,,	1·27
Rural household income group	*1·08*
2 500–2 999 pesos	1·08

C. National parameters

Accounting rate of interest (ARI)	= 12 per cent
Consumption rate of interest (CRI)	= 2 per cent ($e = 2$)
	= 10 per cent ($e = 1$)
Premium on savings (S)	= 4 ($e = 2$)
	= 5 ($e = 1$)
Date by which consumption and savings are equally valuable (T)	= 30 years

D. Distributional weights

Annual income per head (pesos)	By region ($e = 2$)										All Philippines	
	I	II	III	IV	V	VI	VII	VIII	IX	X	$e = 1$	$e = 2$
408	0·106	0·250	0·345	0·200	0·190	0·296	0·257	0·323	0·269	0·230	0·305	0·247
600	0·049	0·116	0·160	0·092	0·088	0·137	0·119	0·150	0·124	0·107	0·208	0·114
800	0·028	0·065	0·090	0·052	0·049	0·077	0·067	0·084	0·070	0·060	0·156	0·064
1 000	0·018	0·042	0·057	0·033	0·032	0·048	0·043	0·054	0·045	0·038	0·125	0·041
1 400	0·009	0·021	0·029	0·017	0·016	0·025	0·022	0·027	0·023	0·020	0·089	0·021
1 600	0·006	0·015	0·021	0·012	0·011	0·018	0·015	0·019	0·016	0·014	0·075	0·015

E. Shadow wage rates (SWR) for unskilled labour

I. Rural (assuming competitive wage paid)

Region	SWR/Market wage
II	0·96
III	1·13
IV	0·96
V	1·08
VI	1·12
VII	1·09
VIII	1·07
IX	1·09
X	1·16
All Philippines	*1·08*

II. Urban

Sector	Market wage (pesos per day)	SWR/market wage
Unorganised	6·5	0·9
Organised "normal"	10·0	0·8
Organised "élite"	13·0	0·9

Indirect taxes, being a transfer payment (and hence not a social cost), are ignored. The ratio of the market and accounting consumer price is then the accounting ratio at consumer prices. The commodities shown in Part A of table 1 are classified according to two codes. The 3-digit code corresponds to the classification used in the National Economic Council's 194-sector input–output table.[1] The 2-digit classification corresponds to that used in the 33-sector input–output table derived by the ILO employment mission from the 194-sector table.[2]

---

[1] *The Statistical Reporter* (Manila), Jul.–Sep. 1971.

[2] See ILO: *Sharing in development* . . ., op. cit., special paper 19: "Intersectoral linkages and direct and indirect employment effects".

It should be noted that the accounting ratios for the commodities shown in part A of table 1 (with the exception of rice and palay) are all based on 1965 data. However, as we discuss at length in Appendix C, there are reasons for believing that these ratios did not alter significantly between 1965 and 1973, when Phase I of this study was completed. In the second phase, which ended in 1974, we did not attempt to recalculate these accounting prices for 1974; however, at least for petroleum-based products the relative accounting prices rose after 1973. This would, however, tend to reinforce the practical conclusions of our study[1] about the social desirability of using men rather than petroleum-consuming machines on road construction in the Philippines.

Part B of table 1 summarises the estimates we have made of the consumption conversion factors for the Philippines as a whole, for the various regions, and for selected urban and rural household income groups. These can be used directly to revalue the consumption accruing to the relevant group into "all-Philippines" accounting values by dividing the relevant value of consumption at market prices by the appropriate consumption conversion factor.

Parts C and D of table 1 summarise the estimated value of various national parameters and give our estimates of distributional weights for marginal income increases of different income groups on two alternative assumptions about the elasticity of social marginal utility ($e = 1$ and $e = 2$).

Part E of table 1 summarises various estimates we have made of the shadow wage rates (SWR) for different occupational groups on varying assumptions.

The ways in which all these estimates were derived are discussed at length in Appendix C. It may be noted here that the accounting prices summarised in table 1 may also be used directly to evaluate other investment projects in the public sector in the Philippines (subject to the qualification that changes may have occurred in the relative prices of traded goods since 1973).

ACCOUNTING PRICES FOR THE INPUTS OF ALTERNATIVE TECHNIQUES

In this section we determine the accounting or shadow prices of the specific inputs required for the evaluation of the alternative techniques for road construction described in Chapter 2. In deriving these specific shadow prices, we make use of the accounting ratios derived in table 1.

The major inputs are capital equipment and labour. Others include carabaos and carts, fuel, cement and hand-tools. It should be noted that the accounting prices we present have been derived specifically for the Capas–Botolan road alternatives. We have used the same accounting prices to evaluate the concrete paving and road hauling alternatives. For these latter alternatives, project-specific shadow prices—particularly for labour—should ideally be used.

Equipment

We require an estimate of the rental rate per hour for equipment at accounting prices. First, we estimate the accounting price of the piece of equipment when it is

---

[1] See Chapter 4.

new. This will be the c.i.f. price plus the accounting costs of port handling, transport, and so on. A breakdown of the costs of a number of items of equipment by these categories were available and is given in Appendix C. From this the c.i.f. cost is a "tradeable" cost at par. Port handling, wholesale margin and other fees (excluding taxes) were deflated by the accounting ratio for wholesale trade of 1·23 (see table 1A). This yields the accounting price of the piece of equipment when new. Say it is P_e^a pesos.

Next, we obtain the market value of fuel and other materials per hour required to operate the machine. This is converted into accounting values by applying the accounting ratio for products of petroleum and coal (1·14, from table 1A). This gives us the value of fuel at accounting prices $V_f^a = F/A_f$.

The third step is to estimate the annual repair and maintenance costs which would keep the machine intact (M). The implicit depreciation assumption is that the machine remains intact till the year T, and then falls to pieces.

The accounting rental rate per hour for the equipment can then be derived as follows. An estimate is made of the average lifetime of the equipment (T) and the average annual machine-hours of service it can provide (H). For it to be worth while to buy the equipment when new at an accounting price of P_e^a pesos, the discounted present value of the net social profit (at accounting prices) of the equipment over its lifetime must be at least equal to its accounting price when new, the discount rate used being the ARI of 12 per cent (see table 1C).[1]

In Appendix D we derive the shadow rental rates for the equipment to be used on the alternative techniques. The main technical uncertainty was as regards the estimates of the lifetime of equipment and the annual repairs and maintenance costs to keep the equipment intact.[2] Hence lower and upper bounds were placed on these estimates by the engineers associated with the study. The resulting upper and lower bounds for the shadow rental rates for each piece of equipment are given in table 2. The last column of the table lists the market rental rates for the items currently used by the Bureau of Public Highways.

---

[1] The relevant formula can be derived as follows. Let the accounting hourly rental rate to be charged be R. Then the annual net social profit of the equipment will be

$$[R - (F/A_f) - (M/A_m)H]$$

and the present value of this social profit, discounted at the ARI, must equal the accounting price of the equipment when new, P_e^a pesos. Hence

$$P_e^a = \sum_{t=0}^{T} \frac{H[R - (F/A_f) - (M/A_m)]}{(1 + ARI)^t}$$

Table 54 derives the annual shadow rental rates for the equipment to be used on the alternative techniques (Y) from the above equation, using a simple transformation where

$$Y = P_e^a \bigg/ \sum_{t=0}^{T} \frac{1}{(1 + ARI)^t}$$

[2] The latter were estimated by the engineers as a percentage of the border price of the equipment, and hence are tradeable at par (i.e. the estimates of M/A_m were made as a percentage of P_e^a pesos).

Table 2.   Market and shadow prices of equipment
(pesos)

Type of equipment	Total daily rentals		
	At shadow prices		At market prices
	Lower bounds	Upper bounds	
Bulldozer D6	496·0	664·0	592·0
Bulldozer D8	1 073·0	1 457·0	1 145·0
Payloader, 1·5 m³	328·0	456·0	413·0
Grader	464·0	640·0	426·0
Pneumatic roller	202·0	290·0	323·0
Road roller	242·0	346·0	258·0
Truck, 8 tons	139·0	203·0	184·0
Water tank, 6 m³	211·0	315·0	201·0
Farm tractor, 60 hp	131·0	195·0	144·0
Crane, 15 tons	386·0	538·0	639·0
Diesel hammer	199·0	303·0	176·0
Air compressor, 370 cfm	72·0	112·0	125·0
Concrete mixer, 4/50C	28·0	44·0	101·0
Vibrator, 7 hp	7·0	12·0	13·0
Concreter	191·0	271·0	401·0

Labour

The Capas–Botolan road is situated in Region IV (Central Luzon). From Appendix C, table 52, it appears that only 43·3 per cent of the total labour force in this region is employed in agriculture. This is below the average for the Philippines as a whole and is accounted for by the presence of a number of small towns in the region. Though the plan is to use purely rural labour, it is possible that the increased (and fairly large) demand for labour which the labour-intensive method would create could draw in some unskilled labour from the small regional urban areas. We neglect the latter complication, and assume that it will be built entirely by local rural labour.

The road was planned to be built between October 1973 and January 1974,[1] that is, during the palay harvesting season. From local inquiries at Camp O'Donnell (where the project was to start and from where it would draw most of its labour) it appeared that there was not much unemployed labour during the agricultural season. These inquiries also revealed that the average daily wage paid to harvesters in Camp O'Donnell was 6 pesos. We can take this as representing the market value of palay output forgone by employing local labour during the harvesting season (see Appendix C). The accounting ratio for converting the market value of palay in Region IV into "all Philippines" accounting prices is 1·04 (see Appendix C, table 31). Hence the shadow wage rate (SWR) for local labour *which is paid the palay harvester's wage of 6 pesos per day* is

$$\text{SWR}_1 = 6/1·04 = 5·77 \text{ pesos.}$$

[1] In fact, the construction of the road did not begin till January 1974. Nevertheless in this evaluation we assume that it was built between October and January.

Alternatively, the labourers could be paid the minimum daily wage for public works projects (8 pesos); this, in fact, is the assumption made in the market price calculations. In this case, in addition to the output forgone of $5 \cdot 77$ pesos per day, the labourers will also be receiving an extra $8 - 6 = 2$ pesos of extra income. This entails both social costs and benefits. The cost is the resource cost of providing the worker with the extra goods and services which he will consume out of his rise in income: if the worker consumes, say, a proportion C_w of his income, the economy will have to incur costs of $2 \cdot 00 C_w$ pesos at market prices to provide him with the increase in consumption. The value of this at *accounting* prices is given by applying the consumption conversion factor for Region IV, which is $1 \cdot 36$ (table 1B). From the data on household expenditures of farm labourers it appears that only $0 \cdot 1$ per cent of their expenditure is on taxes, and that on average their savings are negative. We can therefore plausibly assume that $C_w = 1$. Hence the accounting value of the social costs of increased consumption is $2/1 \cdot 36 = 1 \cdot 47$ pesos.

Not all this increase in the labourers' consumption, however, is a social cost, for (as we argue in Appendix C) there will be some social benefit from increasing the consumption of "poor" workers. In deriving this social benefit, as we have argued, it is necessary to take account of both intertemporal and intratemporal income distribution. This is done by applying the composite distributional weight d_f for the lowest income group (408 pesos per head), to which farm labourers belong. Table 1D (neglecting inter-regional income distribution) gives:

(i) $d_f = 0 \cdot 305$ (where $e = 1$); and

(ii) $d = 0 \cdot 247$ (where $e = 2$).

Adding this to the accounting cost of the output forgone of $5 \cdot 77$ pesos, we get our second estimates of the SWR, *assuming that the labour will be paid the minimum daily wage of 8 pesos*, of:

$$\text{SWR}_{II} \text{ (i)} = 5 \cdot 77 + 1 \cdot 02 = 6 \cdot 79 \text{ pesos (when } e = 1\text{);} \quad \text{and}$$

$$\text{(ii)} = 5 \cdot 77 + 1 \cdot 11 = 6 \cdot 88 \text{ pesos (when } e = 2\text{).}$$

As the values of both SWR_{II} (i) and (ii) are close to each other (thereby implying that the value of the distributional parameter e does not make much difference to our estimates), we shall take a common approximation value of $\text{SWR}_{II} = 7$ pesos per day.

We next relax our assumption that inter-regional income distribution does not matter. The appropriate composite distributional weight d_f will then be that for the 408 pesos per head income group in Region IV. From table 1D this is $0 \cdot 2$; hence, the social cost of the "extra" consumption will now be $1 \cdot 47(1 - 0 \cdot 2) = 1 \cdot 18$, and the SWR, when project labour is paid 8 pesos per day and income distribution in all three dimensions is taken into account, is

$$\text{SWR}_{III} = (5 \cdot 77 + 1 \cdot 18) = 6 \cdot 95 \text{ pesos (when } e = 2\text{).}$$

This again is close to 7 pesos per day; thus the SWR when labour is paid 8 pesos per day does not seem to be sensitive to the particular assumptions made about the distributional weights.

Finally, we consider the possibility of using seasonally unemployed labour in road construction. This is because, although the road was meant to be built towards the end of the palay season, it was built mainly during the agricultural off-season. Presumably this would not lead to any forgone agricultural output, and hence the social cost of this element of the SWR would be zero. However, given that the supply price of labour even during the off-season will not be zero, a positive wage will have to be paid to the labourers to induce them to work, these wage payments (if they equal the supply price) being the necessary compensation to the workers for their disutility of effort. If we assume that the average competitive wage rate over the year as a whole measures the payments to be made for these "costs", we can take the figure of 5·5 pesos per day (for male labourers) which was obtained from local inquiries at Camp O'Donnell. The accounting value of these payments will be the cost of an equivalent amount of consumption that will have to be provided. The latter accounting costs are obtained by applying the consumption conversion factor for Region IV, which is 1·36 (table 1B). This yields our fourth SWR:

$$\text{SWR}_{IV} = 4 \cdot 04 \approx 4 \text{ pesos},$$

which is the shadow daily wage rate, assuming that *seasonally unemployed labour will be employed and be paid a competitive wage of 5·5 pesos per day, and private disutilities of effort are valued socially at par.*

We next relax the assumption that private disutilities are valued socially at par.[1] In this case there is no output forgone, nor is there any social cost on account of the disutility of effort, when seasonally unemployed labour is used on road construction. However, the project authorities will still have to pay the workers their supply price of 5·5 pesos per day, and this will still entail a resource cost at accounting prices of 4 pesos on account of the "extra" consumption these payments will entail. However, on distributional grounds as before, the net social cost of this extra consumption will only be $4(1 - d_{/IV})$ pesos. From table 1D we have $d_{/IV} = 0 \cdot 20$ (for $e = 2$) and hence the estimate of

$$\text{SWR}_V = 4(1 - 0 \cdot 20) = 3 \cdot 20 \text{ pesos},$$

which is the SWR, *assuming seasonally unemployed labour is used in road construction and paid its supply price of 5·5 pesos per day, but private disutilities are not socially valued.*

Table 3 summarises the five SWRs we have estimated for the Capas–Botolan road on alternative assumptions.

Skilled labour

A number of semi-skilled operatives will be required to operate the various equipment items, as well as in managerial functions. We have used the SWR ratio for the normal organised sector of $\text{SWR} = 0 \cdot 8W$ (where W is the market wage— see Appendix C) to derive the accounting costs of skilled labour on the alternative techniques.

---

[1] See Lal: "Disutility of effort ...", op. cit., for reasons why it may be valid to relax this assumption.

Table 3.   Summary of shadow wage rates (SWR) for the Capas–Botolan road

Alternative	Characteristic	SWR (pesos per day)
SWR$_I$	Otherwise employed local labour is paid the competitive local palay harvester's wage of 6 pesos per day	5·77
SWR$_{II}$	Otherwise employed local labour is paid the minimum wage of 8 pesos per day and taking account of intratemporal and intertemporal income distribution:	
	(a) when $e = 1$	6·79
	(b) when $e = 2$	6·88
SWR$_{III}$	Otherwise employed local labour is paid the minimum wage of 8 pesos per day and taking all three distributional dimensions (including inter-regional) into account and assuming that $e = 2$	6·95
SWR$_{IV}$	Seasonally unemployed local labour is paid its supply price of 5·5 pesos per day and private disutilities of effort are socially valued	4·04
SWR$_V$	Same as IV, except no social value is placed on private disutilities of effort and all three distributional dimensions are taken into account	3·20

Carabaos and carts

Carabaos can be hired for about 4 pesos per day in the Camp O'Donnell area. As carabaos are used extensively during farm operations this figure can be taken to represent the value marginal product (and hence output forgone) of carabaos at market prices. Assuming that the output forgone consists of palay, we can use the accounting ratio for palay in Region IV of 1·04 (Appendix C, table 31) to derive the accounting cost of a carabao as $4 \div 1·04 = 3·85$ pesos per day.

For carts, local inquiries revealed that a new cart costs about 400 pesos and lasts on average for about five years. Again using an argument analogous to that used to derive the rental rate of equipment, and assuming that annual depreciation is about 5 pesos, we assess the total annual cost of a cart as approximately 120 pesos.[1] If we next assume that the cart is used on average for about 240 days in a year, we obtain a daily rental rate for a cart at accounting prices of 0·50 pesos.

---

[1] Suppose that

P = yearly flow of *net* "output" from carts (assumed to be in palay equivalent values at market prices);

A_{pIV} = accounting ratio for palay in region IV;

K = cost of a new cart;

T = lifetime of carts; and

ARI = accounting rate of interest.

Then

$$K = P/A_{pIV} \sum_{t=1}^{T} \frac{1}{(1 + \text{ARI})^t}.$$

Substituting the values

K = 400 pesos; $A_{pIV} = 1·04$ (from Appendix C, table 31); and

ARI = 12 per cent (from table 1C),

we have

$P/1·04 = K/3·605$; and

P = $400 \times 1·04/3·605 = 115·39$ pesos.

The daily accounting cost of a cart and carabao, at accounting prices, will therefore be $3·85 + 0·5 = 4·35$ pesos.

Cement

The accounting ratio from table 1A is $1·26$, and this value has been used to convert market into accounting values.

Hand-tools

The accounting ratio for iron and steel foundry products (item 107 in Table 1A) of $1·11$ was used to convert market into accounting values.

OUTCOME

4

In this chapter we outline the outcome of our study of labour-capital substitution in road construction in the Philippines. The first section gives in brief the results of the calculations of the social and market profitability of the alternative techniques. In the next section we discuss the problems posed by the likelihood of there being differential gestation lags in building roads by labour-intensive or capital-intensive methods. In the third section we examine various policy issues concerned with the implementation of socially desirable labour-intensive techniques in road construction in the Philippines.

PROFITS

Capas–Botolan road

Table 4 summarises the results (of which full details are given in Appendix D) of pricing the inputs for the three alternative sets of techniques described in Chapter 2. For the shadow prices two sets of values are given. These correspond to the lower and higher limits of the wage/rental ratio. The upper and lower limits of the rental rates were discussed in the last chapter. The upper and lower SWRs used correspond to (a) *the high SWR of 7 pesos per day*, on the assumption that otherwise employed labour is used and paid a daily wage of 8 pesos, which is above the supply price of labour in the area during the harvest season (this SWR value, as we noted in the last chapter, takes account of all income distribution effects); and (b) *the low SWR of 4 pesos per day*, which corresponds to the assumption that seasonally unemployed labour is used and paid its supply price, which reflects the private disutilities of effort which are socially valued at par.[1]

The low wage–high rental and high wage–low rental combinations then give the likely range of the social costs of building the road by alternative techniques.

---

[1] We have not taken the lowest SWR estimate, which assumes that labour's disutilities of effort are not socially valued, as this is controversial. However, the relative costs of the alternative techniques if this assumption is made can be readily determined by revaluing the labour component of the three alternatives. The total costs are thus for the *ex ante* estimates: capital-intensive, 266,217 pesos per km; labour-intensive, 123,158 pesos per km; and modified labour-intensive, 136,675 pesos per km.

Table 4. Costs of alternative techniques for building the Capas–Botolan road (5·76 km) (pesos)

Technique	Market prices		Shadow prices			
			Low wage–high rental		High wage–low rental	
	Ex ante	Revised	Ex ante	Revised	Ex ante	Revised
Labour-intensive	1 282 317		706 448		996 754	
(Cost per km)	(222 624		122 647		173 048)	
Capital-intensive	1 429 018	1 251 233	1 533 057	1 376 700	1 198 208	1 082 932
(Cost per km)	(248 093		266 156		208 022)	
Modified labour-intensive	1 262 359	1 056 798	783 839	633 346	1 023 361	813 246
(Cost per km)	(219 160		136 083		177 667)	

Source: Appendix D.

From table 4 it can be seen that even at market prices, for the *ex ante* estimates, both the alternative labour-intensive methods are cheaper than the capital-intensive one, and their relative superiority improves with shadow pricing. However, whereas at market prices the modified labour-intensive method is cheaper than the labour-intensive method, this ranking is reversed with shadow pricing.

Table 4 also shows that, for the two alternative methods (capital-intensive and modified labour-intensive) for which field data were collected and revised estimates derived, at market prices and on both shadow pricing assumptions the modified labour-intensive method is again cheaper than the capital-intensive method.

Average gravel road

Table 5 summarises the social evaluation of the two alternative techniques for building an average gravel road for both the *ex ante* and the revised estimates. Once again, at both market and shadow prices the modified labour-intensive method is cheaper than the capital-intensive method.

Table 5. Costs of alternative techniques for building an average gravel road (1·0 km) (pesos)

Technique	Market prices		Shadow prices			
			Low wage–high rental		High wage–low rental	
	Ex ante	Revised	Ex ante	Revised	Ex ante	Revised
Capital-intensive	136 926	118 880	143 841	131 250	112 047	102 663
Modified labour-intensive	122 809	100 685	79 751	62 127	100 102	77 976

Source: Appendix D.

Table 6. Costs of alternative techniques for concrete paving of roads (per 1 000 m²) (pesos)

Technique	Market prices	Shadow prices	
		Low-wage–high rental	High wage–low rental
Capital-intensive	2 137	1 737	1 504
Labour-intensive	2 153	1 709	1 725

Source: Appendix D.

Concrete paving of roads

Table 6 summarises the results for the two alternative techniques for undertaking this task. The capital-intensive method is marginally cheaper at market prices. The results with shadow pricing are interesting. They show that, assuming a high shadow wage and a low rental rate, the superiority of the capital-intensive method improves, but that with a low shadow wage and high rental rate the labour-intensive method is marginally preferable.

This underlines two important aspects of deriving and appraising labour-intensive techniques for road construction. First, extreme caution is necessary in recommending particular labour-intensive techniques, which may be technically feasible and would also generate more employment, until their social costs have been properly evaluated. Second, accurate shadow price estimates can be crucial in determining the relative social desirability of particular techniques. Part of the uncertainty about shadow price values (e.g. for the rental rates) is due to the lack of adequate technical data concerning utilisation rates, repair and maintenance costs and lifetimes of equipment under local conditions. The systematic calculation and evaluation of this technical data is a prerequisite both for forming an over-all judgement about the desirability of labour-intensive techniques in general and for enabling accurate social cost estimates to be made when specific alternative techniques are being appraised in practice.

The uncertainty concerning the shadow wage rate really relates to the use of different types of labour in road construction. The social cost of labour can vary considerably (as our estimates show), depending upon the type of labour, the time of the year it is utilised and the region from which it is drawn. Not surprisingly, other things being equal, the lower the social cost of labour the more likely it is that otherwise unemployed labour will be utilised. However, as our discussion in Appendix C emphasises, it is essential to be very careful in forming a judgement about the social cost of labour. The temptation must be resisted of assuming that most labour to be used on road construction will be otherwise unemployed, because this assumption is unlikely to be generally valid.

Excavation and hauling of fill material

Table 7 summarises the results of using our two limiting sets of shadow prices on the relative social desirability of the alternative methods for excavating and hauling.

Table 7.   Relative desirability of alternative methods of excavating and hauling

Haul distance (m)	Cheapest method
At market prices	
0–25	Bulldozer
25–250	Carabao-drawn cart (hand-loaded)
250–5 000	Farm tractor/trailer combinations (hand-loaded)
5 000 +	Dump-truck/payloader
At shadow prices	
High wage–low rental:	
0–250	Carabao-drawn cart
250–3 200	Farm tractor/trailer combinations
3 200 +	Dump-truck/payloader
Low-wage/high rental:	
0–500	Carabao-drawn cart
500–3 400	Farm tractor/trailer combinations
3 400 +	Dump-truck/payloader

Source: Appendices B and D.

Thus, on both sets of shadow price assumptions, the more capital-intensive methods using bulldozers and various other motorised and bulldozer/scraper combinations are not socially profitable. The result of shadow pricing is therefore to eliminate the bulldozer combinations, as compared with the results at market prices. However, the order in which the other three techniques appear as socially desirable with increasing haul distance remains unchanged.

GESTATION LAGS

There is one hitherto neglected aspect which may be of importance in determining the economic viability of labour-intensive techniques. We have so far assumed that the given task for which alternative techniques are devised can be undertaken in the same time by either equipment- or labour-intensive techniques. It may be felt that this assumption is unrealistic. In fact, many engineers argue that one of the advantages of using equipment-intensive rather than labour-intensive methods lies in the shorter time that they require to complete a given task in road construction—the reason being that large labour groups are unwieldy to manage, and in some cases men may well be getting in each other's way. Machines, then, may be more efficient, in terms of the time taken to complete the tasks.

We can take account of this argument in a rough and ready manner only, for we have not made any attempt to quantify the benefits from either the Capas–Botolan or an average gravel road, as this would have been a formidable task in itself. However, some notion of the order of magnitude of these benefits is essential if we are to quantify the relative social costs of differing gestation lags with alternative techniques. But we can ask an alternative question, the answer to which would provide some indication of the effects of such differential lags. This question can be posed as follows.

Suppose the benefits (at accounting prices) from the length of an average gravel road which can be built in a year by equipment-intensive methods are just sufficient to make the net present value of the *net* benefit stream positive at the ARI. Given that the same benefit stream would flow if the same length of road were built by labour-intensive methods, how much more time can be spent, using labour-intensive techniques, for the net present value of the *net* benefit stream of this alternative to be positive at the ARI?

This question is analysed formally in Appendix E. The conclusions depend upon the various assumptions we have made about the shadow wage/rental ratio and alternative assumptions about the time over which the costs of the labour-intensive alternative can be spread. It is more reasonable to assume that these are spread equally over the number of years it takes to build the road than that they are concentrated in the first year (the two alternative assumptions analysed in Appendix E). On the former assumption we find that the break-even times (t) under the labour-intensive method, but having no greater or lesser effects on social welfare than the capital-intensive alternative for the low wage–high rental and high wage–low rental assumptions, are: $t = 10$ years (low wage–high rental); and $t = 4$ years (high wage–low rental). The particular assumptions made about the shadow wage/rental ratio, and the spreading of costs on the labour-intensive method, are thus crucial in deciding how relatively "time-inefficient" labour-intensive techniques can be and yet remain economically viable. This is clearly likely to be an important aspect of the choice of technique in road construction, in which both technical judgements (about the feasibility of spreading costs over time) and economic judgements (about relative shadow prices) are likely to be extremely important; but our results above suggest tentatively, that, for roads which can be built by seasonally unemployed labour, it may be desirable to use labour-intensive techniques, and even to take much longer over building the road, by building it during the agricultural slack season. This conclusion could be of some importance for rural road construction.

It should, however, be noted that our estimate of the net benefits forgone by not building a road on time is in a sense a "minimum" estimate, as it is derived on the assumption that the capital-intensive alternative just breaks even, and also that the welfare value of a physically identical "output" delivered at two different points of time is the same. In general, however, the welfare value of the same road at different points in time will differ. Other things being equal, the greater the over-all "atemporal" social benefits from building a road, the greater the social opportunity costs of forgoing these benefits by postponement; hence the relative social desirability of a labour-intensive road project with a longer gestation lag would be lower. To make these calculations it is necessary to form some estimate of the net social benefits from a particular road. We have not made any such attempt in this study, and as a result our conclusion that it is desirable to use labour-intensive methods on roads where seasonally unemployed labour can be utilised is tentative. However, for a number of rural gravel roads, the over-all benefits in terms of passenger time saving, of savings on reduced congestion and vehicle operating costs (which are the more commonly adduced benefits of roads), and so on, may be relatively small as compared with those for major arteries. For such roads the social present value of the resource savings resulting from using seasonally unemployed labour may not be offset by a large reduction in the social present value of the benefits forgone due to the longer gestation lags which the use of labour-intensive techniques might entail.

Furthermore, there is some evidence[1] to suggest that labour-intensive methods need not necessarily lead to longer gestation lags in road construction than capital-intensive methods. For example, the Chinese recently built a 174-km hill road in Nepal in six years using labour-intensive methods, whereas another project using capital-intensive methods took five years to build 109 km of road in the relatively easier *terai* area in Nepal.

The work on the Chinese project was so organised as to be carried out simultaneously at various places along the project. The normal sequence of operations common to capital-intensive projects was thus eschewed in favour of a method which was geared to labour-intensive techniques and which, as a result, did not lead to any increase in the gestation lag of labour-intensive road construction. The period of construction was, moreover, arranged to coincide with the agricultural slack season.

It may therefore be premature to assume that the use of labour-intensive techniques would necessarily increase gestation lags in road construction in the Philippines. To the extent that the larger input of labour which may be required can be spread over the length of the road, by increasing the number of sections on which construction is begun, the over-all time taken for building the whole road may not be any longer than with capital-intensive techniques—even though, on any given section of the road, machines work faster than men. Obviously, spreading large numbers of men over a wide terrain will imply all sorts of organisational problems in managing men, which we shall discuss in greater detail in the following section.

POLICIES

Having determined both the technical feasibility and the social desirability of using intermediate techniques in certain tasks in road construction, we are left with the problem of devising suitable public policies which will lead to the implementation of the socially desirable technique. These relate to the design of appropriate fiscal remedies, as well as to other measures to overcome the institutional biases and managerial problems militating against the adoption of appropriate labour-intensive techniques in road construction in the Philippines.

Taxes and subsidies

Clearly, if the socially desirable technique is also the privately most profitable technique to use at market prices, there are no problems of implementation. Such problems arise only if socially profitable techniques are privately unprofitable. The problem of implementation then differs according to whether the project is to be carried on within the public or the private sectors.

The public sector case is straightforward. Even though the actual payments and receipts of the public sector project will be those at *market* prices, nevertheless the actual choice of projects and techniques must be made at shadow or accounting prices. It should be noted, however, that these shadow prices are (as emphasised in Chapter 3 and Appendix C) "second best" prices, which take account of all the relevant constraints on the economy, as well as the general

---

[1] In unpublished ILO research.

equilibrium effects of actual payments and receipts at market prices on aggregate social welfare. As we have also explicitly taken account of the fiscal constraint in deriving the intertemporal shadow prices (in particular the premium on savings), and as this appears in the shadow prices we have determined, there is no further need to take account of any other fiscal constraint. If it is felt that there is such a need, the original derivation of the intertemporal shadow prices could not have been correct and would clearly need to be revised. If, however, it is agreed that these intertemporal accounting prices (in particular the values of s and the ARI) are correct, no further account need be taken of a fiscal constraint. The public sector should implement all projects with a positive net present social value (NPSV) at the ARI.

The solution to the problem of a departmental budget constraint, which prevents it from choosing all projects with a NPSV at the ARI, is also well known.[1] In this case of capital rationing, the correct rule is to "select projects in order of their present value per unit of constrained cost until the cost constraint is exhausted".[2] Again, no special implementation problems arise because of divergences between social and private profitability.

The problem of implementation therefore exists only in the case of private sector investment decisions, where at market prices a project is privately unprofitable, whereas at accounting prices it is socially profitable. One solution to the problem is to take such projects into the public sector. Failing this, the obvious solution is to institute a system of taxes and subsidies given by the divergence between the accounting and market prices of the various goods and services, such that the tax-subsidy-inclusive market prices are equated to the shadow or accounting prices.[3]

For the various alternative techniques considered in this study, we have already estimated the divergence between the shadow and market prices for different items of equipment and types of labour. These differences give the appropriate levels of the relevant taxes and subsidies. In table 8 we have computed the tax on the rental rate of different types of equipment which would equate the social and tax-inclusive market rental rates of equipment. Given the large number of distortions in the domestic price structure (largely as a result of the trade control system), there is no single rate of tax which would be appropriate for all equipment. This underlines the importance in the medium term of bringing some of the actual market prices into line with their accounting prices, particularly for traded goods, by removing the distortions in the relative prices of these goods caused by highly differentiated tariff structures. The distortion in the labour market will nevertheless remain in dual economies,[4] and to correct this our estimates suggest a 10 to 20 per cent subsidy to the wage bill of unskilled labour in the organised sector.

---

[1] See S. A. Marglin: "Economic factors affecting system design", in A. Maass et al.: *Design of water-resource systems* (London, Macmillan, 1962); R. Layard (ed.): *Cost–benefit analysis* (Harmondsworth, Penguin, 1972).

[2] Layard, op. cit., p. 53.

[3] Such tax-subsidy schemes can be made self-financing. Given the existence of current taxes and subsidies, there will be some combination of the two which will establish the tax-subsidy-inclusive factor price ratio that is socially correct, without creating fiscal problems for a government. See I. M. D. Little: "Trade and public finance", in *Indian Economic Review*, Oct. 1971.

[4] Given the assumptions of wage rigidity and surplus labour.

Table 8. Taxes and subsidies (T) on equipment rental rates to equate their market and social values
(percentage)

Type of equipment	Shadow rental rate assumption	
	Lower bounds	Upper bounds
Bulldozer D6	−16·22	12·16
Bulldozer D8	−6·29	0·48
Payloader, 1·5 m³	−20·59	10·41
Grader	8·92	50·23
Pneumatic roller	−37·47	−10·22
Road roller	6·21	34·10
Truck, 8 tons	−24·46	10·32
Water tank, 6 m³	4·97	56·71
Farm tractor, 60 hp	9·03	35·41
Crane, 15 tons	−39·60	−15·81
Diesel hammer	13·06	72·15
Air compressor, 370 cfm	−42·40	−10·40
Concrete mixer, 4/50 C	−72·28	−56·44
Vibrator, 7 hp	−46·16	−7·70
Concreter	−52·37	−32·42

Note: T is derived from $R_m(1 + T) = R_s$ where R_m is the market rental rate and R_s the shadow rental rate given in cols. 11, 12 and 13 of table 54.

For the particular case of road construction, however, the implementation problems we have discussed above are not likely to be of much importance, because most road construction is done under public auspices and these projects can therefore be considered in the same way as any other public sector project. There may, however, be some problems of policing when the cost of the socially optimal technique at market prices is higher than that at shadow prices. In such cases, if the work is subcontracted out to private contractors as is the case in the Philippines, the contractor—whilst receiving the payments for the high market cost (but low social cost) technique—might nevertheless actually employ the low market cost technique, pocketing the difference between the payments the Department of Public Works, Transportation and Communication makes to him and the costs he incurs in building the road. However, as it is possible in most road construction tasks actually to specify the equipment–labour content and as it is fairly easy to see if, for instance, machines are being used instead of carabao-drawn carts and men for hauling fill material, the policing of the specified socially optimal technique should not be too difficult.

Institutional biases

In the ILO study on road construction in Iran[1] it was found that contract bidding procedures and imperfections in the equipment rental market created a

---

[1] ILO: *Roads and redistribution . . .*, op. cit.

bias against the adoption of socially desirable, labour-intensive road construction techniques. We shall now endeavour to ascertain to what extent similar biases operate in the Philippines.

Legacies of the past

The training of most Philippine engineers, either directly or indirectly, in American capital-intensive techniques predisposes them against considering what are felt to be technologically inferior or backward labour-intensive techniques. Furthermore, the effect of a vast supply of construction equipment left in the Philippines by the United States, in the shape of surplus war supplies, and of the reparations received from Japan has been that the private costs of equipment-intensive methods have been low in the past; moreover, there has been no incentive to adopt or adapt more appropriate techniques as a result of any limited availability (or high cost) of road construction equipment.

Administrative and bidding procedures

In the Philippines the Government builds roads itself through the Department of Public Highways and by contracting out the work to private contractors.

The distribution of the work (i.e. between the Department of Public Highways and the contractors) is not clear-cut. Smaller jobs are generally handed down to engineering districts, while larger jobs are put up to bids by contractors. However, given the uneven spread of the supply of contracting services, it may not be possible to obtain any bids from private contractors in remote regions. In such cases the project is undertaken by the Department. It may be noted that only contractors who have been through a prequalification test are allowed to bid (see below). While the bids are coming in, the Department prepares its own cost estimate, but this is not finalised until the last sealed tender has been received. It is only at this stage, and before the sealed tenders are opened, that the Department's own estimate for the project is agreed upon within a departmental bidding committee. This committee prepares its estimate partly on the basis of its records of past bids, partly on the chances of getting contractors to bid for projects in remote regions (which in turn depend upon the supply of regional contracting services), and partly on adjustments for any rise in the prices of materials, men and/or machines. The tenders are then opened and compared with the Department's estimate. If the bids are within ±10 per cent of that estimate, the lowest bid is accepted and the project is contracted out. If, however, none of the bids falls within these limits, the Department undertakes the job itself (although in some cases it may ask for rebids and also revise its own estimate). The principles on which these last two decisions are made are not clear and obviously depend upon the judgement of the members of the departmental committee.

The contract lays down the specifications of the road as regards quality and various technical details but it contains no specification regarding the equipment–labour mix to be used for any particular task. The new guidelines drawn up by the Department of Public Highways for provincial and other departments do mention that labour-intensive methods should be used wherever feasible—but such methods are not specified in the contract. The contract also stipulates a date for the completion of the project, but no specific penalty is laid down if this stipulation is not met.

Prequalification test

Only those contractors who have been approved by a prequalification committee are allowed to bid for projects. The main criterion applied by this committee is that the contractor should have an adequate stock of his own equipment (or access to it through adequate funds for renting equipment) which, in the committee's judgement, is necessary to undertake a road construction job. This means that, normally, only those contractors who already have quite a large stock of machines are able to bid for road construction projects. Given that they are already committed to this stock of machines, they will naturally try to maximise their use. This leads to an equipment-intensive bias in the methods of construction they are willing to consider. This impression was reinforced during personal interviews with a number of contractors, who were very reluctant even to consider labour-intensive alternatives for particular tasks.

Time

The desire of the authorities and (possibly) of the contractors to finish the task in the shortest time possible, coupled with the stipulation that the project is to be completed by a particular date, also tends to increase capital intensity because, as we argued above, there is likely to be a feeling that the use of labour-intensive methods will increase the gestation lags of projects. From the social viewpoint, if there are differential gestation lags, the social costs of this delay have to be set against the possible social benefits in terms of any reduction in the social costs of construction by more labour-intensive methods. As we emphasised earlier in this chapter, it is by no means clear that the social costs of delays outweigh in all cases the possible benefits of using more appropriate techniques, as is implied by the current emphasis on completing projects in the shortest possible time. Furthermore, as is demonstrated by the Nepalese experience cited earlier, labour-intensive techniques do not necessarily entail longer gestation lags. If innovative organisational methods are used and traditional sequential methods of road construction are replaced by simultaneous methods of spreading the construction work over several sections of the road, the current impression that labour-intensive methods would be time-consuming may be erroneous for a number of types of road. More precise data on gestation lags with alternative techniques are required before firm judgements on this issue can be formed. Nevertheless, there may still be a case for selectivity in stipulating different gestation lags for different types of road project, depending upon the factors discussed in Chapter 2.

Managing men

If the social desirability of more labour-intensive technology in road construction is established, this will imply the need to mobilise fairly large bodies of men to build the typical road. This is likely to create serious problems of management. We have not made any attempt to quantify the possible diseconomies which may result from this source, but it is an aspect which could be of great importance, and one which does worry project authorities when they are considering the substitution of men for machines.

One problem is that of effective co-ordination. In the context of the distinction between product- and process-centred industries discussed in Chapter 1 and Appendix A, it may be noted that the problem of co-ordination is likely to be greater in product-centred industries. This is because, as Hirschman has noted,[1] in these industries the operations are likely to be "operator-paced" rather than "machine-paced". The latter operations impose their own inexorable rhythm and discipline, and hence the problem of external co-ordination is greatly reduced. As a result, for unskilled labour, productivity rates could be higher if labour's operations are machine-paced rather than self-paced. This introduces another area of uncertainty when determining labour productivity in different road operations, for both the ability to co-ordinate and the will to submit to discipline in large labour forces will differ from country to country, and possibly from region to region, since these aspects are likely to be dependent upon various specific institutional and cultural factors. These factors further underline the need for extreme caution in advocating the global adoption of labour-intensive techniques in road construction.

We can nevertheless delineate the tasks of co-ordination in a largely labour-intensive project. For instance, advance planning will be important to ensure that the necessary resources will be in the right place at the right time, bearing in mind that these resources will be mostly human and have more complicated and unpredictable characteristics than machinery. This will require greater attention to problems of motivation when organising, co-ordinating and controlling their activities.

Motivation is essentially based upon two considerations: financial reward, and confidence in the management. The attainment of financial reward through the operation of the *packquiao* or piece-rate system is common throughout the Philippines, and this method results in the highest productivity (provided that the *packquiao* rates are equitable). Relative labour productivity has been found to be higher with a piece-rate system in India too, and the Chinese also used this system rather than daily wage rates to obtain the highest labour productivity on the road they built in Nepal. Confidence in management is a function of management's competence in planning and administering the work, its fair dealing and consideration for workers' welfare and its ability to communicate ideals and objectives to the workforce. Thus, on the Chinese road in Nepal where, at the peak, some 1,600 labourers were employed at one time, the supervision of the work by Chinese engineers was extremely close, with 15 to 20 technicians working in each subdivision.

A further problem which tends to compound the difficulties of co-ordination and motivation is that unskilled labour in the construction industry is normally employed on a non-permanent basis. This makes it difficult, as regards the workers' welfare, to equate an extra job created in construction with, say, an extra job created in industry because of the differing degree of uncertainty attached to the future income stream the worker receives from the two jobs. It also means that the problem of co-ordination often needs to be tackled afresh with each batch of

---

[1] "It appears likely that an untrained labour force will perform better in machine-paced operations, not so much because of a tendency towards slacking when the machine does not compel the work, as because machine-paced operations provide for steadiness of pace and regular brief rest periods which the inexperienced self-paced worker has difficulty in observing. In general, it is well known that output per worker varies far more in operator-controlled than in machine-controlled operations." (A. O. Hirschman: *The strategy of economic development* (New Haven, Conn., and London, Yale University Press, 1958), p. 145.)

55

untrained casual labour. These problems could be overcome to some extent by attempting to create a more permanent labour force in construction, possibly in the public sector. This would necessitate a greater long-term commitment to planned expenditure in the sector. However, as construction normally seems to bear the brunt of changes in public expenditure induced by short-term demand management considerations, the above policy would imply surrendering the use of this instrument, at least to some extent. Nevertheless, in the Philippines, where infrastructure development is particularly important for future development,[1] a commitment to maintain a particular level (or rate of growth) of expenditure on construction would not seem to be too onerous.

---

[1] See ILO: *Sharing in development* . . ., op. cit.

APPENDICES

"ESSENTIAL" TECHNICAL PROGRESS AND INTERMEDIATE TECHNOLOGY

In Chapter 1, in our discussion of the possibility of substituting labour for capital, we emphasised that it was essential that labour-intensive techniques should not be inferior to existing capital-intensive techniques. We noted that in the past, as technical progress had occurred mainly in the capital-abundant, labour-scarce, developed countries, the aggregate production function had not shifted smoothly outwards (as is often implied in many neoclassical theories); only certain parts of the relatively capital-intensive portions had done so. However, the case for encouraging the currently developing countries to invest scarce resources in inventing new non-inferior labour-intensive techniques (to compensate for the historical bias of localised technical progress) depended crucially on the extent to which existing labour-intensive techniques were dominated by the advanced technique, on the resource requirements for improvement and on various intertemporal parameters such as the time horizon of planners.[1] This approach did not seem very promising, therefore, in judging the scope for the substitution of labour for capital in particular sectors or industries in developing countries.

There is, however, an alternative approach based on certain insights due to Marx,[2] and more recently echoed in Hirschman's writings,[3] which appears to be more promising. This would attempt to answer the following question: "What are the sectors or industries in which technical progress in the past has resulted in an 'essential' substitution of labour for capital, so that any reverse substitution of labour for capital must imply technical inefficiency?" This will leave us with sectors where what seems to be technical progress is more likely to have been purely the substitution of capital for labour *along* a given isoquant in response to changing factor prices. The identification of sectors where capital-intensive "technical progress" has not been "essential" will therefore provide us with some indication of the areas where the efficient reverse substitution of labour for capital may be feasible without the invention of completely new labour-intensive techniques being necessary. A historical approach is likely to be particularly useful here, and it is for this reason that Marx's writings on technology are particularly illuminating.

Marx distinguishes between "machines" and a "system of machinery", and is particularly concerned with trying to understand, first, what distinguishes the tools of handicraft from machines; second, what distinguishes "the co-operation of a number of machines of one kind from a complex system of machinery";[4] and third, how the role of

---

[1] See Atkinson and Stiglitz: "A new view of technological change", op. cit., pp. 576–577.

[2] K. Marx: *Capital*, Vol. 1, Chapters XIV and XV. All references are to the edition published by Lawrence and Wishart (London, 1970).

[3] Hirschman: *The strategy of economic development*, op. cit., Ch. 8.

[4] Marx, op. cit. p. 378.

labour changes as we move from what he calls the stage of "manufacture" (which is essentially organised handicrafts permitting specialisation and division of labour) to that of a "real machinery system".

From the outset Marx is conscious of a vital distinction in the process of manufacturing different products and the differing technological responses this calls forth. These differences are present even at the organised handicraft stage (or "manufacture" stage, in Marx's terminology) and arise "from the nature of the article produced. This article either results from the mere mechanical fitting together of partial products made independently, or owes its completed shape to a series of connected processes and manipulations."[1]

It is in particular for the latter type of what would nowadays be called "process-centred industries"[2] that a "system of machinery", in Marx's terminology, is far superior to the process of "manufacture", as it reduces the costs of "the incessant transport of the article from one hand to another, and from one process to another",[3] which is an essential feature of process-centred industry. Once "a real machinery system" is introduced, "we have again the co-operation by division of labour that characterises manufacture; only now, it is a combination of detail machines. [As] the collective machine . . . becomes more and more perfect, the more the process as a whole becomes a continuous one. . . . In Manufacture the isolation of each detail process is a condition imposed by the nature of the division of labour, but in the fully developed factory the continuity of those processes is, on the contrary, imperative."[4]

In modern terminology for process industries, modern methods enable a considerable saving in circulating (working) capital, as compared with the handicraft stage. The introduction of a "system of machinery" in these industries is therefore the equivalent of substituting relatively cheaper fixed capital for working capital. This substitution has in fact been identified by Sir John Hicks as the distinguishing feature of the Industrial Revolution.[5] The reason why fixed capital became cheaper than circulating capital was the fall in interest rates and the greater availability of liquid funds in the first half of the eighteenth century in England.[6] Moreover, once the substitution of fixed for circulating capital began, there was (as Hicks notes) an impetus to scientists to invent machines to make machines. It was this latter development which ensured the technological superiority of advanced methods in process industries, for the machines made by machines were more accurate and cheaper (because of scale economies) than the first generation of machines built by hand.[7] The economies of scale in process industries have moreover proved to be continuing, because of the particular technological feature of most of these

---

[1] Marx, op. cit., p. 342.

[2] This is the term proposed by Hirschman, op. cit., p. 147. His distinction between such industries and what he terms "product-centred" industries is clearly foreshadowed by Marx.

[3] Marx, op. cit., p. 344.

[4] ibid., pp. 379–381.

[5] J. R. Hicks: *A theory of economic history* (Oxford, Clarendon Press, 1969), pp. 142 ff.

[6] ibid., pp. 79, 94 and 144.

[7] Thus Hicks states: "The first generation of machines were made by hand with some assistance from water power; they were expensive, because of the highly skilled labour needed to construct them, and they were not very accurate because of their continued reliance upon this human element. Cost was reduced, and accuracy improved, in the second generation—the machines that were made by machines. This is well explained by the author of the chapter on machine tools in the *History of technology* (Oxford, 1964–68, Vol. 4, p. 417): 'Machine tools make it possible to work metal objects of great size and to shape metals with an accuracy unattainable by hand. Moreover, the high speed of working with machine tools makes commercially practicable processes which, even if mechanically possible, cannot be performed economically by hand. . . . The invention and development of machine tools was an essential part of the industrial revolution'. It may indeed be that we should be right to recognise it as the essential part." Hicks, op. cit., p. 147.

processes, namely that plant costs per unit of output necessarily decrease with output.[1] Most of these processes are carried out or connected through various three-dimensional structures, whose costs of construction are related to surface area, whereas their capacity is linked to their volume. Thus, for instance, the construction costs of a cylinder (which is a common shape in most chemical processes, in the form of pipes, vats, tanks, etc.) will vary with its area (given by $2\pi r(r + l)$ where r is the radius and l the length), whilst its capacity (and hence output) will vary with its volume (given by $\pi r^2 l$). For such industries, therefore, the capital-using bias of modern techniques is likely to be irreversible, and more labour-intensive alternatives (for instance, by reducing the scale of plants) are likely to be inferior.

We are, however, still left with the first set of industries distinguished by Marx whose products result from "the mere mechanical fitting together of partial products made independently". These are the industries which Hirschman labels "product-oriented", such as "construction and much of metalworking, as well as . . . most service industries [in which] work is not patterned around one or several key technical processes. As a result, sequences are far less rigidly compelled, it is impossible to identify any one process as central, and tasks are typically defined in terms of their *direct* contribution to the achievement of the goal—the final product—rather than in terms of the roles performed in different phases of the production process."[2] However, the scope for labour-capital substitution in Hirschman's "product-centred industries" category is not likely to be uniform, for, as we have seen,[3] in certain of these industries (e.g. metalworking) the economies of scale and the accuracy attainable by modern methods are likely to be irreplaceable. Marx's narrower definition of these product-centred industries is therefore likely to be more suitable for finding industries in which there may be technically efficient ways of substituting men for machines.

To determine the areas in which such substitution may be feasible, it is illuminating to determine the causes for the initial substitution of machines for men in these more narrowly defined "product-centred" industries. Again Marx is incisive.[4] He argues that, whilst the machines in these industries use implements and tools which are similar to those used by handicraftsmen,[5] the productivity of these machines is likely to be higher; for the number of implements that a man "can use simultaneously is limited by the number of his own natural instruments of production, by the number of his bodily organs. . . . The number of tools that a machine can bring into play simultaneously is from the very first emancipated from the organic limits that hedge in the tools of a handicraftsman."[6] The substitution of such machines for men depends primarily upon the relative productivities and prices of the two.[7]

This suggests that if there are obvious possiblities of efficient reverse technical substitution of men for machines, it is likely to be in "product-centred" industries in the Marxian sense, and even there primarily in the tasks where the machines used are "a more or less altered mechanical edition of the old handicraft tool". The most obvious candidate is the construction industry, which is primarily a "product-oriented" industry in both Marx's and Hirschman's sense, and in which many of the machines used are

---

[1] See G. C. Hufbauer: *Synthetic materials and the theory of international trade* (London, Duckworth; Cambridge, Mass., Harvard University Press, 1966); F. T. Moore: "Economies of scale: Some statistical evidence", in *The Quarterly Journal of Economics*, May 1959; N. Kaldor: "The irrelevance of equilibrium economics", in *The Economic Journal*, Dec. 1972.

[2] Hirschman, op. cit., p. 147.

[3] Fn. 7, p. 60.

[4] Marx, op. cit., pp. 371–374.

[5] These and early machines were, moreover, also handicraft products.

[6] Marx, op. cit., pp. 374 ff.

[7] ibid., pp. 393–394.

PRODUCTIVITY ESTIMATES

B

In Chapter 2 we outlined the various estimates of the productivity of men and machines made by the ILO engineers for this study. This appendix presents these estimates in detail. As noted in Chapter 2, there are two sets of estimates: the *ex ante* estimates made in June 1973, and the revised estimates made after the field experiments conducted on the Capas–Botolan pilot road project in 1974.

SUMMARY OF THE *EX ANTE* AND REVISED PRODUCTIVITY ESTIMATES

Capas–Botolan road

The *ex ante* and revised productivity estimates for the construction of the Capas–Botolan road by (*a*) labour-intensive; (*b*) capital-intensive; and (*c*) modified labour-intensive methods are summarised in tables 9 and 10. The following points should be noted for all these estimates.

(1) Neither estimate includes site overheads, but each does include the costs of junior supervisors, i.e. foreman and *capataz*. It is considered that, whatever method were used, overheads would be of the same order and the cost of extra facilities required for large forces of labour would be balanced by the facilities required for the maintenance and repair of equipment. As such overheads would amount to only about 10 per cent of the total project cost the effect of any minor differences would be minimal.

(2) In the labour-intensive estimates it has been assumed that the *packquiao* system,[1] which is traditional to the Philippines, has been used on the majority of tasks, thereby giving optimum productivity.

(3) On the other hand, the equipment performance figures used are those currently obtaining in the Philippines, and are suboptimal. In general, equipment hire rates are higher and outputs are lower than would be the case in developed countries. The situation in the Philippines is typical of many developing countries, in that during the

---

[1] *Packquiao* system: a form of negotiated communal contract, often paid for on the basis of unit prices. The engineers may offer advice on what would be considered a fair price per unit of work. On the basis of their observations, the associate experts derived *packquiao* rates for the actual construction of the Capas–Botolan road that would enable participants to earn a satisfactory recompense, having due regard to the relaxation needs of their particular tasks. The performance and earnings of workers on the *packquiao* system were observed to be higher than those of daily paid labour.

Table 9. *Ex ante* and revised productivity estimates for the construction of the Capas–Botolan road

Code no. (1)	Description (2)	Quantity (3)	Method [1] (4)	Productivity [2] (5)	Unit cost (pesos) (6)	Total cost (pesos) (7)	Cost per km (pesos) (8)	Wages component Cost (9)	Wages component % of (7) (10)	Equipment component Cost (11)	Equipment component % of (7) (12)	Total man-days [2] (13)
Phase 1: *ex ante* estimates												
100	Clearing and grubbing	22 ha	1	44 m² man-day	2 307	50 754	8 815	43 704	86.1	7 050	13.9	5 256
			2	573 m²/h for D7	2 643	58 150	10 098	6 238	10.7	51 912	89.3	615
			3	222 m²/man-day for clearing / 536 m²/h for D7 grubbing	2 115	46 538	8 082	9 112	19.6	37 426	80.4	1 074
105a	Excavation (average 100 m haul) [3]	160 000 m³	1 and 3	5.0 m³/man-day for excavation and loading / 92.5 m³/man-day for loosening by ploughing / 18.0 m³/day hauling 100 m by bullcart / 139.0 m³/day spreading by bamboo scraper	5.10	816 000	141 716	569 784	69.8	246 216	30.2	57 696
			2	37.5 m³/h for D7 and for grader / 62.5 m³/h for sheepfoot compaction	6.02	963 334	167 304	22 505	2.3	940 829	97.7	2 226
105b	Soft rock excavation [3]	2 982 m³	1	0.59 m³/man-day for excavation and hauling / 11.25 m³/h for compressor drills and blasting	15.20	45 326	7 872	42 246	93.2	3 080	6.8	5 160
			2	75.0 m³/h for D7 levelling	18.24	54 397	9 447	4 839	8.9	49 558	91.1	289
			3	1.5 m³/man-day for excavating load and hauling 30 m by wheelbarrow	15.23	45 415	7 887	21 409	47.1	24 006	52.9	2 442
106	Excavation for structures	790 m³	1	1.13 m³/man-day for excavating backfill and tamping	8.04	6 352	1 111	6 352	100.0	0	0	725
			2	1.7 m³/man-day for excavation / 5.6 m³/man-day for backfilling and tamping	8.00	6 320	1 098	6 320	100.0	0	0	651
			3	1.7 m³/man-day for excavation / 5.6 m³/man-day for backfilling and tamping	6.75	5 332	926	5 332	100.0	0	0	651
110	Foundation fill (5 km)	125 m³	1	3.5 m³/man-day for backfilling and tamping	8.40	1 050	182	300	28.6	750	71.4	36
			2	100 m³/loading 1-1/2 m³ payloader	9.95	1 256	218	458	36.5	798	63.50	55
			3	3.0 m³/man-day for spreading / 7.2 m³/man-day for loading trailer / 4.0 m³/man-day for spreading	8.40	1 050	182	480	45.8	567	54.2	58
111	Overhaul	143 000 station meter [1]	1	24 trips per day per bullcart	0.10	14 400	2 500	7 200	50.0	7 200	50.0	900
			2	60 m³/h for 1.5 m³ payloader	0.14	20 370	3 527	540	2.7	19 830	97.3	45
			3	30 m³/h for 4.5 m³ dump-truck / 24 m³/h haulage capacity of farm tractor with 6 trailers	0.06	8 342	1 448	740	8.9	7 602	91.1	74

No.	Item	Quantity	Col.	Description								
200	Borrow base (5 km)	11 100 m³	1	70 m³/h loading capacity of 1·5 m³ payloader; 35·6 m³/day for spreading by bamboo scraper	10.37	115 155	19 992	25 992	22·6	89 163	77·4	3 005
			2	73 m³/h for 4·5 m³ dump-truck; 72 m³/man-day for loader and trailer	8·28	91 911	15 962	3 651	4·0	88 260	96·0	329
			3	35·6 m³/day for spreading by bamboo scraper	9·59	106 402	18 479	37 896	35·6	68 506	64·4	4 330
405	Concrete	381 m³	1, 2 and 3	0.291 m³/man-day for setting up forms and casting	180·23⁴	68 670	11 926	13 100	19·1	11 416	16·6	1 308
406	Reinforcing steel	34·5 tons	1, 2 and 3	84 kg/man-day	2 300⁴	79 350	13 781	3 600	4·5	290	0·4	412
505	Reinforced concrete pipes	645 m	1, 2 and 3	0·14 m³/man-day for casting; 0·4 m forms/man-day	132·19⁴	85 260	14 809	32 860	38·5	0		3 656
Phase II: revised estimates												
100	Clearing and grubbing	22 ha	2	573 m²/h including pulling down trees for D7; 308 m²/man-day for clearing	2 274·27	50 034	8 689	802	1·6	49 232	98·4	68
			3	1320 m²/man-day for grubbing sugar-cane field	1 139·41	25 067	4 353	21 555	86·0	3 512	14·0	2 352
105a	Excavation (average 100 m haul)	160 000 m³	2	37·5 m³/h for D7; 110 m³/h for spreading by grader; 67 m³/h for compaction by pneumatic roller	5·24	838 391	145 604	24 267	2·9	814 124	97·1	2 078
			3	3·6 m³/man-day for excavation, loading and hauling 10 m by wheelbarrow; 16·5 m³/man-day for excavation, loading and hauling 25 m by steel-scraper; 3·3 m³/man-day for excavation, loading and hauling 125 m by bullcart	4·05	647 818	112 507	416 974	64·4	230 844	35·6	45 680
105b	Soft rock excavation	2 982 m³	2	18 m³/h including 25 m hauling for D8 with ripper; 1·0 m³/man-day for excavation	11·64	34 704	6 027	354	1·0	34 350	99·0	30
			3	1·5 m³/man-day for loading and hauling 25 m with wheelbarrow	17·36	51 780	8 993	48 000	92·7	3 780	7·3	4 987
106	Excavation for structures	790 m³	2 and 3	3·2 m³/man-day for excavation; 5·7 m³/man-day for backfilling and tamping	7·29	5 760	1 000	5 760	100·0	0	0	630
110	Foundation fill (5 km)	125 m³	2	{ for loading and hauling see item 200; 3·0 m³/man-day for backfilling and tamping	8·46	1 058	184	539	50·9	519	49·1	56
			3	3·0 m³/man-day for backfilling and tamping	10·66	1 333	232	588	44·1	745	55·9	62
111	Overhaul	143 000 station meter³	2	{ 60 m³/h for loading 1·5 m³ payloader; 22·5 m³/h for hauling by 4·5 m³ dump-truck	0·13	18 720	3 251	1 140	6·1	17 580	93·9	93
			3	7·8 m³/day per bullcart	0·11	15 594	2 708	8 256	52·9	7 338	47·1	917

Table concluded overleaf

65

Table 9. (contd.)

Technical data		Quantity	Method[1]	Productivity[2]	Unit cost (pesos)	Total cost (pesos)	Cost per km (pesos)	Wages component		Equipment component		Total man-days[2]
Item Code no.	Description							Cost	% of (7)	Cost	% of (7)	
(1)	(2)	(3)	(4)	(5)	(6)	(7)	(8)	(9)	(10)	(11)	(12)	(13)
200	Borrow base (5 km)	11 100 m³	2	{75 m³/h for loading by 1.5 m³ payloader; 9.6 m³/h for hauling by 4.5 m³ dump-truck	6.25	69 286	12 033	6 965	10.1	62 321	89.9	617
			3	73 m³/h for spreading by grader; {16.5 m³/day for excavation and loading by a trailer; 48.7 m³/day for spreading with compscraper	6.86	76 166	13 228	12 377	16.3	63 789	83.7	1 337
405	Concrete	381 m³	2 and 3	0.291 m³/man-day for setting up forms and for casting	180.23[4]	68 670	11 926	13 100	19.1	11 416	16.6	1 308
406	Reinforcing steel	34.5 tons	2 and 3	84 kg/man-day	2 300.0[4]	79 350	13 781	3 600	4.5	290	0.4	412
505	Reinforced concrete pipes	645 m	2 and 3	0.14 m³/man-days for casting; 0.4 m forms/man-day	132.19[4]	85 260	14 807	32 860	38.5	0	0	3 656

[1] Methods: 1 = labour-intensive; 2 = capital-intensive; 3 = modified labour-intensive. [2] Includes materials. [3] 1 station meter = 1 m³ hauled 100 m. [4] Includes materials. [3] 1 station meter = 1 m³ hauled 100 m. [4] Includes cost of loading.
Source: Government of the Philippines, Department of Public Works, Transportation and Communication: *Construction of levees by labour-intensive methods* (Manila, 1972); data from private contractors in the Philippines, the Bureau of Public Highways and the National Irrigation Authority; field observations.

Table 10. *Ex ante* and revised productivity estimates for the construction of the Capas–Botolan road: summary

Method[1]	Man-days of work Per 1 000 pesos	Per km	Total cost (pesos)	Cost per km (pesos)	Wages component Cost	% of (4)	Equipment component Cost	% of (4)	Total man-days
(1)	(2)	(3)	(4)	(5)	(6)	(7)	(8)	(9)	(10)
Phase I: *ex ante* estimates									
1	58·6	13 052	1 282 317	222 702	745 138	58·1	365 165	28·5	75 154
2	6·7	1 645	1 429 018	248 169	94 111	6·6	1 162 893	81·4	9 586
3	56·8	12 452	1 262 359	219 236	694 313	55·0	396 032	31·4	71 701
Phase II: revised estimates									
2	7·2	1 554	1 251 233	217 303	89 387	7·1	989 832	79·1	8 948
3	68·0	10 653	1 056 798	183 536	563 070	53·3	321 714	30·4	61 341

[1]Methods: 1 = labour-intensive; 2 = capital-intensive; 3 = modified labour-intensive.

Source: As for table 9.

postwar era considerable quantities of modern mechanical equipment were brought in without provision being made for the commensurate inputs for training workshop engineers, mechanics and operators, for workshop facilities and for matching procedures for spare parts. In consequence, the working life of equipment is low, as are utilisation rates.[1] Operating efficiency too is low, particularly in the public sector, whose depots are characterised by huge equipment graveyards. Considerable capital investment and a long period of training would be needed to rectify this state of affairs. Even if appropriate action were taken now, it might take a decade to put matters right; and even then the problems of lower efficiency because of the tropical climate would still remain.

(4) Thus, whereas the efficient operation of labour-intensive methods can be optimised in the short term, the achievement of efficient equipment utilisation is an expensive and long-term problem.

Average gravel road

The data from the Capas–Botolan project were suitably adjusted to arrive at productivity estimates for an average gravel road in the Philippines. The cross-section was taken as being the same as that of the Capas–Botolan road (see figure 1), and the assumption was made that the earthworks and some other items on the Capas–Botolan road were twice the national average. Tables 11 and 12 summarise the resulting *ex ante* and revised estimates for such a road.

Concrete paving of roads

For this operation the ILO engineers substituted labour-intensive hand-placing methods for the capital-intensive method with a concrete-paving machine (concrete finisher). In the labour-intensive method a wooden beam between two side-frames was employed. The engineers obtained data for the two techniques from two existing projects in the Philippines. In both cases concrete was mixed in central batching and/or truck mixers, so that the cost and quality of the concrete delivered to the worksite were the

---

[1] See section on "Equipment utilisation" below.

Men or machines

Table 11. *Ex ante* and revised productivity estimates for the construction of an average gravel road, per km at market prices

Item code no.[1]	Quantity	Method[2]	Unit cost (pesos)	Cost (pesos)	Man-days	Method[2]	Unit cost (pesos)	Cost (pesos)	Man-days
		Phase I: *ex ante* estimates				Phase II: revised estimates			
100	3·5 ha	2	2 643	9 251	98	2	2 274·27	7 960	11
		3	2 115	7 403	171	3	1 139·41	3 988	374
105a	14 000 m³	2	6·02	84 292	195	2	5·24	73 360	18
		3	5·10	71 400	5 048	3	4·05	56 700	3 997
105b	260 m³	2	18·24	4 742	25	2	11·64	3 026	3
		3	15·23	3 960	213	3	17·36	4 514	435
106	70 m³	2	8·00	560	58	2 and 3	7·29	510	56
		3	6·75	473	58				
110	10 m³	2	9·95	100	5	2	8·46	85	5
		3	8·40	84	5	3	10·66	107	5
111	12 500 station meter	2	0·14	1 750	4	2	0·13	1 625	8
		3	0·06	729	7	3	0·11	1 375	80
200	1 930 m³	2	8·28	15 980	57	2	6·25	12 063	107
		3	9·59	18 509	753	3	6·86	13 240	
405	33 m³	2 and 3	180·23	5 948³	113	2 and 3	180·23	5 948³	113
									232
406	3 tons	2 and 3	2 300	6 900³	36	2 and 3	2 300·00	6 900³	36
505	56 m	2 and 3	132·19	7 403³	317	2 and 3	132·19	7·403³	317

[1] For explanation of code numbers, see table 9.   [2] Methods: 2 = capital-intensive; 3 = modified labour-intensive.   [3] Includes materials.

Table 12. *Ex ante* and revised productivity estimates for the construction of an average gravel road, per km at market prices: summary

Method[1] (1)	Cost (pesos) (2)	Man-days (3)	Wages component Cost (4)	Wages component % of (2) (5)	Equipment component Cost (6)	Equipment component % of (2) (7)
Phase I: *ex ante* estimates						
2	137 926[2]	908	8 963	6·5	113 044	82·0
3	122 809[2]	6 721	64 617	52·6	43 274	35·2
Phase II: revised estimates						
2	118 880[2]	674	8 457	7·1	95 487	80·3
3	100 685[2]	5 639	51 841	51·5	33 908	33·7

[1] Methods: 2 = capital-intensive; 3 = modified labour-intensive.   [2] Includes materials.

Table 13. Concrete paving of roads by labour-intensive and capital-intensive methods

Item	Method		
	Labour-intensive		Capital-intensive	

Item	Labour-intensive		Capital-intensive	
Surface area:	24 855 m²		173 993 m²	
Volume:	(24 855 m² × 0·23 m =) 5 717 m³		(173 993 m² × 0·23 m =) 40 018 m³	
Time:	72 days		229 days	
Daily output:	$\frac{5717}{72} = 79 \cdot 4$ m³/day		$\frac{40\,018}{229} = 175$ m³/day	
	$\frac{24\,885}{72} = 345$ m²/day		$\frac{173\,993}{229} = 760$ m²/day	
Cost of equipment (pesos):				
	1 concrete vibrator	(72 × 40 pesos) 2 880	1 concrete finisher	(9 × 25 × 401 pesos) 90 225
	1 water truck	(36 × 201 pesos) 7 236	2 concrete vibrators	(18 × 25 × 40 pesos) 18 000
	1 concrete saw	(72 × 116 pesos) 8 352	1 water truck	(9 × 25 × 201 pesos) 45 225
	1 compressor	(18 × 290 pesos) 5 220	2 concrete saws	(9 × 25 × 116 pesos) 26 100
			1 compressor, 500 cfm	(4·5 × 25 × 290 pesos) 32 625
		23 688		212 175
Wages (pesos per 8-hour day):				
	1 const. foreman	(72 × 14 pesos) 1 008	1 const. foreman	(250 × 22·5 pesos) 5 625
	1 const. carpenter	(72 × 13 pesos) 936	2 operators	(225 × 18 pesos) 8 100
	1 surveyor	(72 × 12 pesos) 864	5 utility operators	(225 × 15 pesos) 16 875
	1 truck driver	(72 × 12 pesos) 864	10 masons	(225 × 21 pesos) 47 250
	1 lab. technician	(72 × 10 pesos) 720	10 labourers	(225 × 12 pesos) 27 000
	1 auditor checker	(72 × 10 pesos) 720	10 carpenters	(225 × 21 pesos) 47 250
	4 survey aids	(72 × 10 pesos) 2 880	3 helpers	(225 × 12 pesos) 8 100
	3 asst. operators	(72 × 10 pesos) 2 160		
	30 labourers	(72 × 8 pesos) 17 280		
	4 carpenters	(72 × 10 pesos) 2 880		
		30 312		160 200
	Total cost (equipment plus wages)	54 000	Total cost (equipment plus wages)	372 375
Costs per m³ (pesos)	9.44		9.31	
Equipment per m³ (pesos)	4.14		5.30	
Wages per m³	5·30 ~ 56 per cent		4·00 ~ 43 per cent	
Man-days (47 × 72)	3 384		(370 × 25 =) 9 250 (12-h day) × 1·5 = 13,875 normal days	
Man-days per m³	0.59		0.347	
Man-days per m²	0.136		0.080	
Costs per 1 000 m² (pesos)	2 173		2 140	
Man-days (ratio of labour-intensive to capital-intensive)	1.7		1.0	

69

same. The relevant data, together with the costs of the alternative methods at market prices, are given in table 13. The figures apply only to the placing and finishing of the concrete, and are exclusive of the cost of the concrete delivered to the site.

Excavation and hauling of fill material

The engineers also experimented with alternative methods of excavating and hauling fill material over various haul distances up to 10 km (see figures 2–6). Only the revised estimates are reported, as there was not a great deal of difference between them and the *ex ante* estimates.[1] Figure 2 gives the output per hour for hauling fill material from 0 to

Figure 2.   Hauling of fill material: output of various types of bulldozer

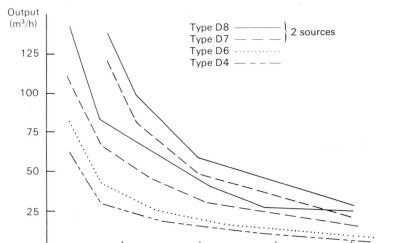

Haul distance (m)

100 m with different types of bulldozer. Figure 3 gives the output per 8-hour day for hauling fill material from 0 to 300 m with carabao-drawn carts.[2] Figure 4 gives the output per hour for hauling fill material from 200 to 1,200 m through the combined use of carry-all scraper and D8 tractor. Figure 5 gives the output per 8-hour man-day of hauling fill material from 0 to 90 m with a modified steel scraper. Figure 6 gives the output per 8-hour man-day of excavating and loading. These alternatives were costed at market prices. The costs of excavating and hauling fill material by the different methods are shown in figures 7 and 8. The labour and equipment content for hauling 1,000 m^3 per 8-h day by the alternative methods is shown in figures 9 and 10.

---

[1] Sources: United States Army engineering book of 1944, used by the Bureau of Public Highways; private contractors.

[2] See United Nations, Economic Commission for Asia and the Far East: *Earthmoving by manual labour and machines*, Flood control series, No. 17 (Bangkok, 1961; Sales No.: 61.II.F.4); Spence Geddes: *Estimating for building and civil engineering works* (London, Newnes–Butterworths, 5th ed., 1971); Department of Public Works, Transportation and Communication: *Construction of levees by labour-intensive methods*, op. cit.; Danish engineering sources.

Figure 3. Hauling of fill material: output of carabao-drawn carts

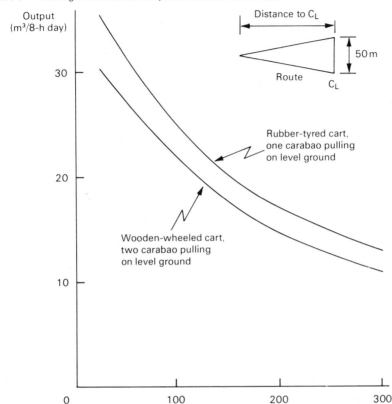

Note: Output figures are for a team of one driver and two labourers per cart, each cart carrying 0·3 m³ of sand, with a density (dry) of 92 lb/cu. ft.

Easy digging in cohesionless Pasig-Potrero sand.

The figures allow for watering the carabao, and a mean rise to the dyke between zero height and maximum height of the dyke (5 m). An interference allowance has also been made on short hauls. Achievement of the above outputs should earn a 25 per cent bonus.

Figures 7 and 8 show that at current market prices the most economical combinations for excavating and hauling are as follows:

Haul distance (m)	Cheapest methods
0–25	Bulldozer (the differences are marginal and could disappear at shadow prices)
25–250	Carabao-drawn cart, hand-loaded
250–5 000	Tractor/trailers, hand-loaded
5 000 +	Dump-truck/payloader

EXPERIMENTAL PRODUCTIVITY DATA FROM THE CAPAS–BOTOLAN ROAD

In this section we give details of the results obtained by the ILO engineers from their field experiments. The following pages show the recorded productivities of men and

Figure 4.   Hauling of fill material: output of carry-all scraper and D8 tractor (8-h/day)

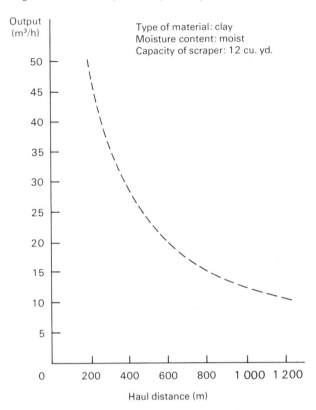

machines under the alternative methods. In interpreting these productivity estimates one should note that productivity is affected by: (a) soil type, length of haul and nature of the ground; (b) the need to bathe carabao regularly, when methods using these animals are adopted (the distance from the workplace to the nearest watering place therefore affects their productivity); (c) the method of payment of labour, i.e. whether the basis is daily pay, task work or the *packquiao* system; and (d) the ambient temperature and humidity (the best results are obtained where workers are on piece-work and can start in the cool of the day at first light). In general, these points have been taken into account in the productivity studies described below.

In the field experiments productivity data on the following activities were collected and analysed, using continuous time or activity sampling techniques:

(1) Clearing and grubbing.
(2) Hand excavation in bulk.
(3) Hand excavation for culverts and drains.
(4) Hand-loading.
(5) Hauling by wheelbarrow.
(6) Hauling by carabao-drawn cart.
(7) Excavation and hauling by carabao-drawn scraper.
(8) Watering of roadway by carabao-drawn tanker.
(9) Hauling by dump-truck and payloader.

Figure 5. Hauling of fill material: output of modified steel scraper

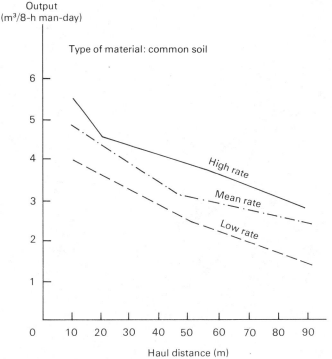

Source: Bureau of Public Works: *Bulletin* (Mar. 1959).

Most of the observations were made on a section of the road reserved for experimentation under the supervision of the ILO engineers. On this section, work methods and gang sizes were first studied, and adjusted where necessary to improve efficiency. Productivity studies were then carried out under three methods of payment of labour, coded by the World Bank as follows: (1) daily paid; (2) task work; and (3) piece-work (corresponding in this context to the *packquiao* system). Workers elsewhere on the site operated under a daily paid system. Where it was possible to compare identical jobs carried out under different systems of payment, it was observed that productivity was highest and earnings greater under the *packquiao* system. The production figures derived and used in the revised case studies were those obtaining under this system of payment. In all cases these figures are the average output over the full working day.

Observations on site indicated that adequate relaxation was taken by the labour force. The output figures given include this relaxation time. Total relaxation time (for all purposes) during the 8-h working day was as high as 45 per cent on some of the heavier operations. This is considered reasonable in view of the severe climatic conditions.[1] Working hours were generally from 7.30 to 11.30 a.m. and from 1.00 to 5.00 p.m. It is considered that still higher productivity could be achieved, and working conditions improved, by working from 5.30 to 11.00 a.m. and from 3.00 to 6.00 p.m.[2]

---

[1] See figure 13 below.

[2] These were the actual working hours determined by the labour force itself during the 1972 pilot project on labour-intensive levee construction.

Figure 6.   Excavation and loading of fill material: output per 8-h man-day

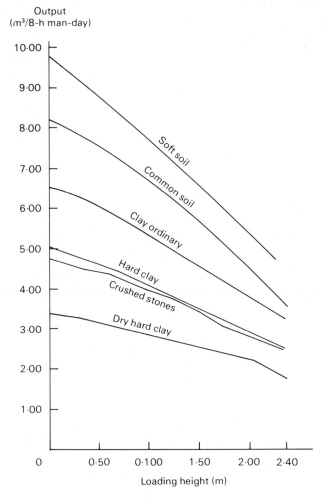

Output
(m³/8-h man-day)

Soft soil

Common soil

Clay ordinary

Hard clay

Crushed stones

Dry hard clay

Loading height (m)

Source: Bureau of Public Works: *Bulletin* (Mar. 1959).

Clearing and grubbing

Clearing and grubbing is the removal and disposal of trees, roots and other debris.

On the Capas–Botolan project vegetation was very light. This operation was heaviest over the first 2 km, where the road passes through sugar-cane plantations.

Work method. The area had been burnt and harvested before the start of the operation, but there remained two or three stumps of sugar-cane per m² with big roots. The area was ploughed four times by carabao-drawn local ploughs. The loosened roots were removed by hand-picking and carabao-drawn comb-scrapers.

Study method. Input was measured through continuous time study, output by measuring the cleared and grubbed area.

Productivity estimates

Figure 7. Cost data for excavating and hauling fill material by different methods at market prices, 0–500 m

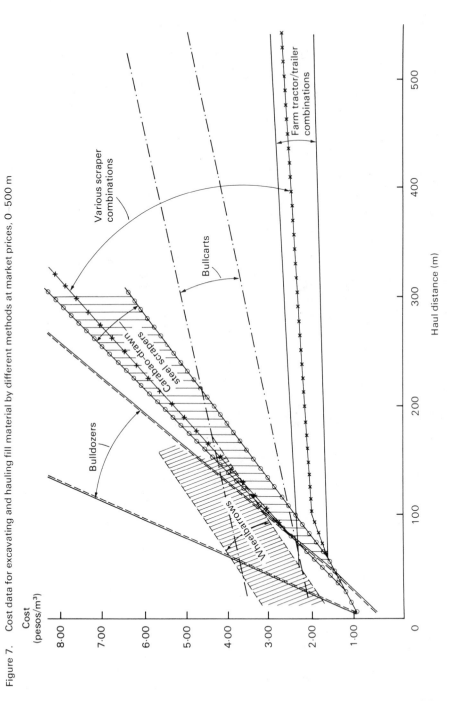

75

Figure 8.   Cost data for excavating and hauling fill material by different methods at market prices, 0–10 km

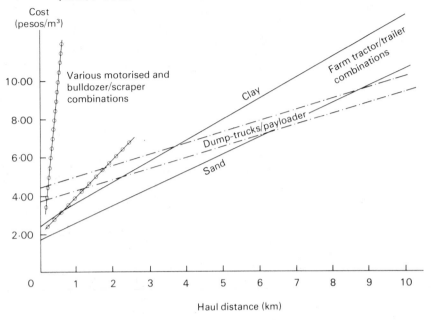

Result. Only one pay method (daily pay) was applied. The following productivity figures were obtained:

Operation	Productivity
First ploughing	250 m²/h
Following ploughing	490 m²/h
Combing	490 m²/h
Hand-picking	250 m²/h

(Distance to water: 25 m)

It was considered necessary to carry out the ploughing operation four times and the combing and hand-picking three times, thus giving a team of two ploughs, one comb-scraper and two labourers for hand-picking. Team productivity was 165 m²/h. For available working time for carabaos at different distances to water, see under "Hauling by carabao-drawn cart" below.

Hand excavation in bulk

By "excavation" is meant the breaking loose of *in situ* (undisturbed) material, usually with a hoe, pickaxe or crowbar. The type of soil influences the choice of tool (e.g. hoes on soft ground, pickaxes and crowbars on hard ground).

The cohesive soils encountered were classified as FIRM, STIFF, VERY STIFF and HARD, corresponding to the World Bank codes 3, 4, 5 and 6 for cohesive soils.[1]

---

[1] See World Bank: *Study of the substitution of labor and equipment in civil construction: Phase II final report.* Staff working paper, No. 172 (Washington, DC, 1974), Vol. II, p. 36.

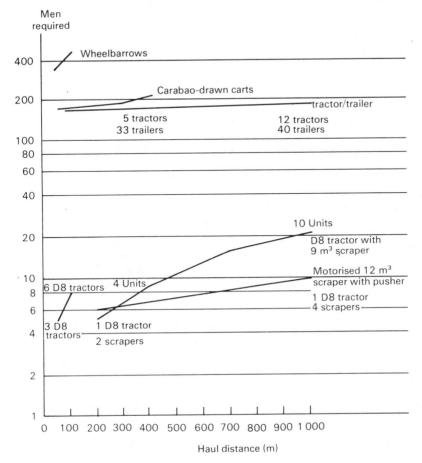

Figure 9.   Labour force required for excavating and hauling 1,000 m³ of fill material per 8-h day by different methods, 0–1,000 m (average figures for common soil)

The average height of cut was 1·10 m (between extremes of 0·75 m and 1·50 m).

Work method. The cut was worked by hoe, pickaxe or crowbar, depending on the type of soil. Excavated material was loaded into wheelbarrows or bullcarts. Stock-piling and double handling were avoided by balancing of the work gangs.

Study method. Cross-counts were used to determine the input man-hours and the activity level (i.e. the ratio of productive to non-productive working time). Output was measured either from the excavated *in situ* volume or calculated through the random weighing of wheelbarrows.

Results. Forty-five studies were undertaken, most of which extended over the whole working day. Daily pay, task work and piece-work (World Bank codes 1, 2 and 3)[1] were

---

[1] See World Bank: *Study of the substitution of labor and equipment in civil construction . . .,* op cit., Vol. II, p. 17.

Figure 10. Labour force required for excavating and hauling 1,000 m³ of fill material per 8-h day by different methods, 0–10 km (average figures for common soil)

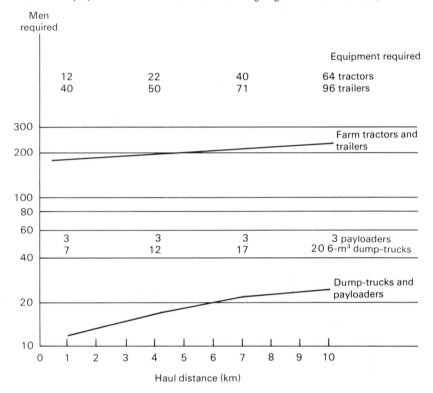

studied. Derived standard productivity under the piece-work (*packquiao*) system was:

World Bank soil code	Firm m³/h
3	2·28
4	1·51
5	0·99
6	0·82

The following table indicates the effect on productivity of the different methods of payment of labour. Productivity is expressed as a ratio, with that for daily paid labour being taken as 1·00.

World Bank pay method code	Productivity ratio
1	1·00
2	1·77
3	1·85

(Soil type: code 5; height of cut: 1·10 m)

Hand excavation for culverts and drains

Excavation for culverts and drains typically comprises loosening the material within the area to be excavated and shovelling the loosened earth out of this area.

Work method. Pickaxes were used to loosen the soil, which was thrown 1 m from the edge of excavation. The average depth of excavation was 1·2 m.

Study method. Input was measured by cross-count or continuous time study. Output was obtained from *in situ* measurements. Observations were made on type 5 soil, using pay method 1.

Result. Derived standard productivity was 0·40 firm m³/h.

Hand-loading

Loading can be described as the transfer of previously loosened material to the wheelbarrow, cart, truck, etc., used for hauling. On the Capas–Botolan project spades were used for loading soil. The means of hauling were wheelbarrows, carabao-drawn carts and dump-trucks.

Work method. When the soil had been loosened, the loaders loaded it on the wheelbarrows or carts with spades. The numbers of loaders per team varied with the method of haul and the distance, but the size of the vehicle and the space around it determined the maximum number of loaders: two or three for carts, five or six for dump-trucks, and one or two for wheelbarrows. The labourer driving the cart or pushing the wheelbarrow did not help in loading.

Study method. Cross-counts and continuous time study were used to determine the input. Output was determined either by sampling (weighing of wheelbarrows) or by total output measurement.

Result. Only negligible differences in productivity were found between the loading of wheelbarrows and carts, but when dump-trucks were loaded a considerable difference was noted. This indicates that the loading heights of wheelbarrows (0·75 m) and carts (1·00 m) are within the comfortable range, whereas in the case of dump-trucks (1·50 m) this range has been exceeded. Derived standard productivity under the *packquiao* system was:

World Bank soil code	Loaded into	Productivity per man
Cohesive (types 3–5)	Wheelbarrows and carts	1·24 firm m³/h
Non-cohesive (type 2-loose)	Wheelbarrows and carts	2·07 firm m³/h
	Dump-trucks	1·42 firm m³/h

The following table indicates the effect on productivity of the different methods of payment of labour. Productivity is expressed as a ratio, with that for daily paid labour being taken as 1·00.

World Bank pay method code	Productivity ratio
1	1·00
2	1·42
3	1·85

(Soil type: cohesive, types 3–5; loading height: 0·75 m to 1·00 m)

Hauling by wheelbarrow

Hauling by wheelbarrow was studied over distances between 20 and 150 m on haul roads classified as "fair" in flat terrain. The wheelbarrows used on the Capas–Botolan project were of a type found in most developing countries, i.e. with a single metal wheel without roller bearings, and with a flat, pan-like container for the load.

Work method. One labourer with a shovel loaded the wheelbarrow and another hauled it. On short haul distances, trials were made with extra wheelbarrows so that one was always ready to be loaded.

Study method. Hauling speeds, cycle times and dumping times were derived through continuous time study. The load per wheelbarrow was obtained either by sampling (random weighing of wheelbarrow plus load) and trip counts, or by total output measurement of *in situ* volume.

Figure 11.   Productivity of wheelbarrows

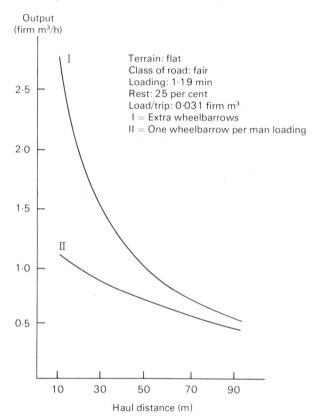

Output
(firm m³/h)

Terrain: flat
Class of road: fair
Loading: 1·19 min
Rest: 25 per cent
Load/trip: 0·031 firm m³
I = Extra wheelbarrows
II = One wheelbarrow per man loading

Haul distance (m)

Speed of wheelbarrow

Distance (m)	Speed when loaded (m/min)	Speed when empty (m/min)
20	89	78
40	87	76
60	85	75
80	83	73

Terrain: flat
Class of road: fair
Weight of wheelbarrow + load: 65 kg

Result. The mean load per wheelbarrow was 0·031 firm m³. The speed differed with the haul distance. The return with empty wheelbarrows was approximately 18 per cent slower than with loaded wheelbarrows. The time for dumping and turning was found to be 0·13 min. With extra wheelbarrows, the time to change wheelbarrows was 0·13 min.

Derived standard productivity with the *packquiao* system was:

Distance (m)	Firm m³/h
20	1·85
50	0·92
90	0·55

Hauling by carabao-drawn cart

The carabao-drawn carts in use had steel-rimmed wooden wheels.

Several factors affect the speed of travel of these carts, particularly the age and condition of the individual carabao. Each animal has its own rate of walking, which varies slightly according to the type of cart, gradient and load. As a result of the observations, a mean rate of travel on firm ground for wooden-wheeled carts of 48·6 m/min was adopted. The speed of the carabao without any attachments was 60 m/min.

It is also necessary to allow time for watering the carabao, each animal again having its own needs. A total allowance of 54 min was made, which was to be taken in four rest periods. To this time was added the time taken in walking from the nearest point on the work route to the watering place. The following table indicates the effect of this watering time on the available production time in one 8-h day (480 min).

Distance to water (m)	Total watering allowance	Available daily production time
25	58 min	422 min
200	81 min	399 min
500	121 min	359 min

These figures have been incorporated in the output columns of table 14 and give the output that can be expected commensurate with good animal husbandry.

Work method. An average time for loading previously loosened material was fixed at 4·9 min, assuming that two labourers were engaged in loading (the total number of workers in a gang depending upon the haul distance). Whilst the carabao was hauling a loaded cart, workers would be loosening material ready for the next haul. Unloading was done by the carabao cart driver; a time of 1·6 min was allowed, this being the mean of observations on site.[1]

Study method. Studies were made on haulage distances up to 400 m. Input was measured by continuous time study. The various carts used on the job had slightly differing capacities, and a mean load carried of 0·315 firm m³ was derived by measuring the actual cut and dividing by the number of loads.

Result. Table 14 shows the daily output of a carabao-drawn cart over various haul distances, with varying distances from the line of haul to the nearest watering place. The pay method was the *packquiao* system.

---

[1] In the 1972 pilot project on levee construction a mean unloading time of 20 s was observed. Here the material was loose, non-cohesive river sand. There was considerably more resistance to the withdrawal of the bamboo mats in the soil types encountered on the Capas–Botolan road. The reduction of this unloading time is under study.

Table 14. Productivity data, hauling by carabao-drawn cart

| Haul distance (m) | Time per trip (min) | | | No. of trips per 8-h day | | | | | | Output in firm m³ per 8-h day (0·315 firm m³ per trip) | | | | | |
| | Loading and unloading | Haul and return | Cycle time | Distance to watering place (m) | | | | | | Distance to watering place (m) | | | | | |
				25	100	200	300	400	500	25	100	200	300	400	500
25	6·5	1·1	7·6	55	54	52	50	48	47	17·3	17·0	16·4	15·7	15·1	14·8
50	6·5	2·1	8·6	49	48	46	44	43	41	15·4	15·1	14·5	13·8	13·5	12·9
75	6·5	3·1	9·6	44	43	41	40	38	37	13·8	13·5	12·9	12·6	11·9	11·6
100	6·5	4·1	10·6	39	38	37	36	35	33	12·2	11·9	11·6	11·3	11·0	10·4
150	6·5	6·2	12·7	33	32	31	30	29	28	10·4	10·0	9·7	9·5	9·1	8·8
200	6·5	8·3	14·8	28	27	26	26	25	24	8·8	8·5	8·2	8·2	7·8	7·5
250	6·5	10·3	16·8	25	24	23	22	22	21	7·8	7·5	7·2	6·9	6·9	6·6
300	6·5	12·4	18·9	22	21	21	20	19	19	6·9	6·6	6·6	6·3	6·0	6·0
350	6·5	14·4	20·9	20	19	19	18	17	17	6·3	6·0	6·0	5·6	5·3	5·3
400	6·5	16·5	23·0	18	17	17	16	16	15	5·6	5·3	5·3	5·0	5·0	4·7
450	6·5	18·5	25·0	16	16	15	15	14	14	5·0	5·0	4·7	4·7	4·4	4·4
500	6·5	20·6	27·1	15	15	14	14	13	13	4·7	4·7	4·4	4·4	4·1	4·1
1 000	6·5	41·2	47·7	9	8	8	8	7	7	2·8	2·5	2·5	2·5	2·2	2·2

Excavation and hauling by carabao-drawn scraper

The construction and use of the scrapers is described in Chapter 2.

Work method. The soil to be worked is previously loosened by ploughing. By varying the pressure on the handles, the operator can load soil as the scraper travels forward. In cutting, the scraper will return empty along a route parallel to the loading run, whereas in side-cutting and burrow, an approximately circular route is followed.

Study method. Continuous time studies were made on the traditional and factory-made (steel) versions of the carabao-drawn scraper, on both non-cohesive sandy soil (World Bank code 2) and firm clay (code 3) over haulage distances ranging from 10 to 100 m, in cutting. The volume excavated was measured from cross-sections at 2 m intervals, measured before and after working. The average loads carried by scrapers were found to be:

Traditional version	0·050 m³
Factory-made (steel) version	0·075 m³

The average speed for hauling (including loading and returning) was 42·9 m/min, the difference between hauling full or empty being insignificant. Unloading time was 0·21 min, and turning and manoeuvring into position took 0·27 min.

Results. Derived standard productivity with the piece-work (*packquiao*) system is given in tables 15 to 17 for the various types of scraper and soil. In these tables, the same allowances for watering carabao have been made as in the case of carabao-drawn carts. Note that studies on non-cohesive soil were curtailed due to the early onset of the rainy season.

Watering by carabao-drawn water cart

Watering is necessary when the moisture content of the soil is too low to ensure optimum compaction. With high temperatures and ploughing, scraping and harrowing, the evaporation loss is high; this was the case on the Capas–Botolan road.

Work method. Three drums, connected with each other, were mounted on a bullcart. The drums were filled with water from buckets. The water was sprinkled on the road through a perforated pipe when a valve was opened. The cart was drawn by a carabao which was itself watered when the drums were being filled.

Study method. Input was measured by continuous time study. Output was derived from the quantity of water used and the area watered.

Result. With a rate of spread of 2 l/m² the derived standard productivity for spreading was 2,676 m²/h (not including filling and transportation). For the whole cycle (filling, hauling, spreading, return and manoeuvring) the following productivity figures were derived:

One-way haul distance (m)	Productivity (m²/h: 2l/m²)
50	1 006
200	706
500	442
1 000	272

The final results are summarised in table 18.

Table 15. Productivity data, earth-moving by carabao-drawn steel scraper (factory-made)
Soil type: cohesive firm (World Bank type 3)

Haul Distance (m)	Cycle time per trip (min)	No. of trips per 8-h day						Output in firm m³ per 8-h day (based on 0.075 m³ capacity)					
		Distance to watering place (m)						Distance to watering place (m)					
		25	100	200	300	400	500	25	100	200	300	400	500
10	1.2	352	344	332	322	310	300	26.4	25.8	24.8	24.0	23.2	22.4
20	1.6	281	275	265	257	248	240	19.3	19.3	18.6	18.0	17.4	16.8
30	1.9	222	217	209	203	195	189	16.6	16.2	15.6	15.2	14.6	14.1
40	2.4	175	172	165	160	155	150	13.2	13.0	12.5	12.0	11.6	11.3
50	2.9	145	142	137	133	128	124	10.9	10.6	10.3	10.0	9.6	9.3
60	3.3	127	125	120	116	112	109	9.5	9.4	9.0	8.7	8.4	8.2
70	3.8	111	108	104	101	97	94	8.3	8.1	7.9	7.6	7.3	7.1
80	4.3	98	96	92	89	86	83	7.4	7.2	6.9	6.7	6.5	6.2
90	4.7	89	87	84	82	79	76	6.7	6.5	6.3	6.1	5.9	5.7
100	5.2	81	79	76	74	71	69	6.1	5.9	5.7	5.5	5.3	5.2

Table 16. Productivity data, earth-moving by carabao-drawn steel scraper (factory-made)
Soil type: non-cohesive loose (World Bank type 2)

Haul distance (m)	Cycle time per trip (min)	No. of trips per 8-h day						Output in firm m³ per 8-h day (based on 0.075 m³ capacity)					
		Distance to watering place (m)						Distance to watering place (m)					
		25	100	200	300	400	500	25	100	200	300	400	500
10	1·2	351	344	331	321	310	299	26·4	25·8	24·8	24·0	23·2	22·4
20	1·6	263	258	248	241	232	224	19·8	19·5	18·6	18·0	17·4	16·8
30	1·9	222	217	209	203	195	188	16·7	16·2	15·6	15·2	14·6	14·1
40	2·2	191	187	180	175	169	163	14·4	14·0	13·5	13·1	12·6	12·2
50	2·5	168	165	159	153	148	143	12·7	12·3	11·9	11·5	11·1	10·7
60	2·7	156	152	147	142	137	132	11·7	11·4	11·0	10·6	10·2	9·9
70	3·0	140	137	132	128	124	119	10·5	10·2	9·9	9·6	9·3	8·9
80	3·4	127	121	117	113	109	105	9·3	9·0	8·7	8·4	8·1	7·8
90	3·7	114	111	107	104	100	97	8·6	8·3	8·0	7·8	7·5	7·2
100	4·1	102	100	97	94	90	87	7·7	7·5	7·2	7·0	6·7	6·5

Table 17. Productivity data, earth-moving by carabao-drawn scraper (traditional type)
Soil type: cohesive firm (World Bank type 3)

| Haul distance (m) | Cycle time per trip (min) | No. of trips per 8-h day | | | | | | Output in firm m³ per 8-h day (based on 0·050 m capacity) | | | | | |
| | | Distance to watering place (m) | | | | | | Distance to watering place (m) | | | | | |
		25	100	200	300	400	500	25	100	200	300	400	500
10	1·1	383	375	362	350	339	326	19·1	18·7	18·1	17·5	16·9	16·3
20	2·0	211	206	199	193	186	179	10·5	10·3	9·9	9·6	9·3	8·9
30	2·2	191	187	181	175	169	163	9·5	9·3	9·0	8·7	8·4	8·1
40	2·4	175	172	166	160	155	149	8·7	8·6	8·3	8·0	7·7	7·4
50	2·9	145	142	137	133	128	123	7·2	7·1	6·8	6·6	6·4	6·1
60	3·3	127	125	120	116	113	108	6·3	6·2	6·0	5·8	5·6	5·4

Table 18.   Productivity data, watering of roadway by carabao-drawn water cart

Haul distance before spreading (m)	Area watered per hour	
	$2 \, l/m^2$	$3 \, l/m^2$
0	1 192	795
50	1 006	682
100	883	598
200	706	478
300	589	398
400	505	342
500	442	300
600	394	267
700	354	240
800	322	218
900	295	200
1 000	272	185

Volume of tank: 500 l
Fixed time: Filling, 4·98 min; emptying, 5·60 min; manoeuvring, 2·00 min
Driver filling tank alone
Carabao resting while tank is filled

EQUIPMENT UTILISATION

The pattern of equipment utilisation in the Philippines is erratic. In Western countries the economic life of an efficiently used piece of equipment is generally taken as 10,000 machine hours. In the Philippines this could range from 20,000 or more to as little as 2,000. New equipment supplied under various foreign aid programmes often do not have adequate support facilities for maintenance, repair and the replacement of parts. Some equipment is also imported reconditioned, and the most productive machine hours have already been taken out. When utilisation is as low as 50 per cent[1] one could expect the working life to be correspondingly longer, but this is not always the case. Cannibalisation for spare parts and deterioration and corrosion due to inclement weather may reduce the lifetime faster than normal wear and tear in use. All these considerations increase the operating costs.

A study was undertaken by the ILO associate experts in October–November 1973 to determine the yearly utilisation of heavy construction equipment and the most common cause for idle time.

Data collection

A number of equipment owners and users, in both the private and the public sector, were contacted. However, very few maintained any reliable records for their machines. Some of the bigger construction companies did have fairly detailed records covering two to three years. The Bureau of Public Highways, the National Irrigation Authority and Provincial Motorpools also had some equipment records. Some of these were unfortunately not so detailed, and in some cases they were less reliable as the working hours were derived from fuel consumption, which is not a very accurate method.

---

[1] See table 19.

Table 19.   Equipment utilisation in the private and the public sector

Item of equipment	Hours worked per month		Percentage of available work time[1]	
	Private sector	Public sector	Private sector	Public sector
Crawler tractor	124·3	84·6	49·7	42·3
Motor grader	118·6	101·5	47·4[2]	50·8[2]
Dump-truck	124·7	110·0	49·9[2]	55·0[2]
Loaders	98·1	124·0	39·2[2]	62·0[2]
Motor scraper	76·5	—	30·6	—
Roller	45·1	50·5	18·0[2]	25·0[2]

[1] Actual working hours as a percentage of expected working hours. For the private sector, 250 hours per month and shift; for the public sector, 200 hours per month and shift.   [2] Less reliable data, as working hours were based on fuel consumption.

Source: Time-cards and operation reports from Philippine contractors, the Bureau of Public Highways and the National Irrigation Authority.

Equipment records (mainly time-cards, operation reports and, in a few cases, equipment costs cards) were consulted, and the actual numbers of working hours and the split-up of the idle time for the studied pieces of equipment were collected. Data for a total of 81 heavy construction machines (876 machine-months with two-shift and 753 machine-months with one-shift operation) were also collected. As much of the construction equipment had previously been reconditioned to a greater or less extent, for most of the machines it was not possible to determine their actual age. However, the collected data on equipment are believed to be representative of the present situation as regards equipment in the Philippines.

Results

As data on utilisation were obtained from both the private and the public sector and as the expected number of working hours differs for the two sectors, the data have been kept separate. It was ascertained through interviews that for private owners and users the expected working time was 10 hours per shift and 25 working days per month. For users in the public sector 8 hours per shift and 25 days per month was the normal working time.

Table 20.   Distribution of recorded idle time for heavy construction equipment[1] (percentage)

Item of equipment	Transport	Waiting for repair/ spares	Under repair/ maintenance	Bad weather conditions	Stand-by	Other	Total
Crawler tractor	3·5	14·3	54·4	16·4	3·6	7·8	100·0
Motor grader	5·5	2·8	40·4	26·4	13·2	11·7	100·0
Dump-truck	0·9	4·4	43·0	20·5	17·9	13·3	100·0
Loader	7·1	13·1	54·9	16·7	0·9	7·3	100·0
Motor scraper	1·8	34·5	42·4	13·2	2·5	5·6	100·0
Roller	0·4	2·2	37·3	18·4	37·6	4·1	100·0

[1] As no significant difference in the distribution could be found between equipment owners in the private and the public sector, the two have been aggregated and presented in the same table.

Source: Time-cards, operation reports and equipment cost cards from Philippine contractors, the Bureau of Public Highways and the National Irrigation Authority.

The number of working days available per month for the private sector would be higher, and thus an even lower utilisation would result.

The data from private sources were, for reasons explained above, collected from large construction companies. These had been using their machines mainly for the construction of dams, where facilities for maintenance and repair were better than on the average road construction site. For road construction the utilisation figures may well be lower than shown in table 19.

Table 20 shows the distribution of the recorded idle time. Only 40–50 per cent of the total idle time is recorded. The distribution of the idle time that is not recorded could be expected to show a higher percentage of "bad weather conditions" than indicated.

Equipment productivity

The output of equipment during its actual working time has not been studied. In the case study the output figures used were those in general use for estimating and scheduling purposes by equipment users in both the private and the public sector in the

Figure 12.   Productivity of crawler tractors (bulldozers) of different make

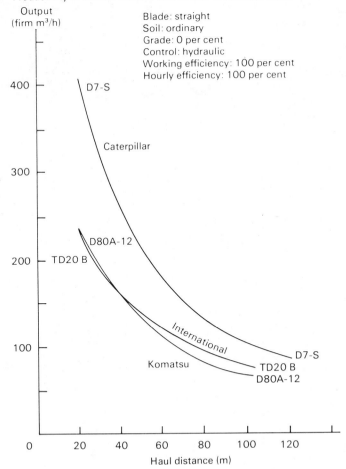

Source: Caterpillar performance handbook: International *Basic estimating*; Komatsu standard production sheet.

Men or machines

Figure 13.   Temperature and relative humidity, Capas–Botolan road, 9 April 1974

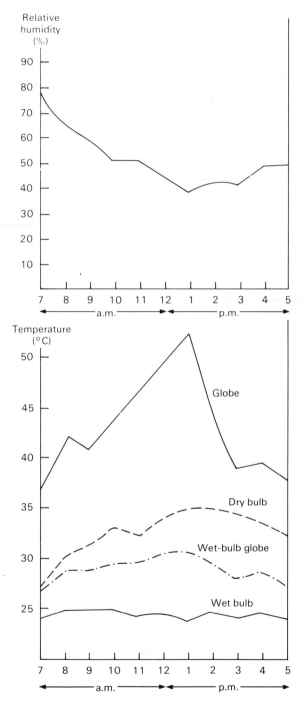

Philippines. In general they are only one-third of the optimum output figures considered attainable by Caterpillar under ideal conditions. Figure 12 gives output figures for bull-dozers of similar types under conditions of 100 per cent working efficiency, as published by three manufacturers of bulldozers, Caterpillar, International and Komatsu.

CLIMATIC CONDITIONS

Figure 13 shows the temperature and humidity on a normal working day during the dry season.

ACCOUNTING PRICES FOR THE PHILIPPINES   C

In the first five sections of this appendix we outline the methods used to determine a comprehensive set of accounting or shadow prices for the Philippines. A brief description of the methodology followed (that of I. M. D. Little and J. A. Mirrlees)[1] was given in Chapter 3. In the final section we give our estimates of the shadow rental rates for various items of equipment used for alternative road construction techniques in the Philippines.

NON-AGRICULTURAL COMMODITIES

In this section we describe how the accounting prices for the major non-traded goods and services in the economy were estimated. In so doing we also had to estimate the accounting ratios for a large number of traded commodities, and the derivation of these accounting ratios is explained as well.

The accounting prices of non-traded goods are given by their costs of production at border prices under the Little–Mirrlees method, the assumption being that any increase in demand for non-traded goods will be met by an increase in supply. If this assumption is invalid, it will be necessary to determine what proportion of the increased demand for the non-traded good is met by reducing its use in consumption and/or production elsewhere. Given this, the appropriate conversion factor for the groups whose consumption is affected can be used to value the social cost of consumption forgone; and the appropriate accounting ratios for the output of the industry or industries whose output is reduced can be used to value the output forgone, by meeting the increased demand for the non-traded good. In what follows, however, we neglect these complications and adopt the Little and Mirrlees assumption that increased demand is met by increased supply.

To determine the social costs of production of non-traded goods, we have made use of the 33-sector input–output table prepared in connection with the ILO comprehensive employment strategy mission to the Philippines.[2] This table was compiled by consolidating the data in the National Economic Council's 194-sector input–output table for 1965.[3]

Traded goods

Of the 33 sectors in the ILO input–output table, 11 were considered to be producing non-traded output. These were sectors 22–32. For each of these sectors the inputs of

---

[1] See Little and Mirrlees: *Social cost benefit analysis*, op. cit.

[2] See ILO: *Sharing in development* . . ., op. cit., special paper 18: "Intersectoral linkages and direct and indirect employment effects".

[3] *The Statistical Reporter*, July-Sep. 1971.

Table 21. Traded and non-traded goods: accounting ratios at producer and at consumer prices

Code number, 33-sector breakdown	Code number, 194-sector breakdown	Sector	Parameter[1]					
			$(1 + t)$	W	A	$(1 - t)$	r	C
I. Traded goods								
17		*Modern consumer goods*	*1·17*	*0·0632*	*1·18*	*0·785*	*0·170*	*1·52*
	035	Processed meat products	1·71	0·0768	1·7347	0·9872	0·1683	1·6441
	039	Preserved vegetables and other preserved fruits	1·54	0·0768	1·5622	0·9872	0·1683	1·5292
	046	Cocoa, chocolate and sugar confectioneries	1·39	0·0768	1·4101	0·9872	0·1683	1·3943
	047	Processed coffee	1·39	0·0768	1·4101	0·9872	0·1683	1·3943
	051	Starch and starch products	1·91	0·0768	1·9376	0·9872	0·1683	1·7901
	053	Other food preparations	1·10	0·0768	1·1159	0·9872	0·1683	1·1485
	054	Distilled and blended spirits and brewery products	1·16	0·0645	1·1741	0·8810	0·2811	1·3502
	056	Soft drinks	1·11	0·0645	1·1235	0·8810	0·2811	1·3073
	057	Cigars and cigarettes	1·19	0·0271	1·1960	0·728	0·1249	1·6488
	059	Textile mill products	1·30	0·0682	1·3166	0·9748	0·1752	1·3344
	060	Knitting mill products	1·11	0·0682	1·1242	0·9748	0·1752	1·1710
	066	Embroidery products	1·11	0·0695	1·1245	0·989	0·2168	1·1587
	067	Other made-up textile goods	1·11	0·0695	1·1245	0·989	0·2168	1·1587
	073	Wood and rattan furniture and fixtures	1·10	0·0588	1·1121	0·957	0·1487	1·1791
	079	Other paper products	1·71	0·0634	1·7304	0·9850	0·1750	1·6401
	085	Leather products	1·07	0·0697	1·0841	0·9791	0·1944	1·1336
	086	Rubber footwear and garments	1·10	0·0606	1·1125	0·9739	0·1414	1·1580
	093	Medical and pharmaceutical preparations	1·25	0·0672	1·2658	0·9905	0·1991	1·2709
	094	Soap and other washing compounds	1·14	0·0672	1·1544	0·9905	0·1991	1·1802
	095	Cosmetic and toilet preparations	1·95	0·0672	1·9746	0·9905	0·1991	1·7796
	097	Matches	1·25	0·0672	1·2658	0·9905	0·1991	1·2709
	118	Household-type appliances	1·78	0·0442	1·7947	0·9860	0·2245	1·6507
	121	Electrical communication equipment	2·47	0·0683	2·5018	0·9838	0·1935	2·1195
	124	Household electrical appliances	1·90	0·0683	1·9244	0·9838	0·1935	1·7639
18		*Traditional consumer goods*	*1·15*	*0·0795*	*1·17*	*0·983*	*0·170*	*1·2004*
	036	Ice-cream products	1·66	0·0768	1·6840	0·9872	0·1683	1·6064
	041	Milled rice	1·15	0·0768	1·1666	0·9872	0·1683	1·1923
	042	Milled maize	1·15	0·0768	1·1666	0·9872	0·1683	1·1923
	044	Bakery products	1·15	0·0768	1·1666	0·9872	0·1683	1·1923
	055	Wines	1·16	0·0645	1·1741	0·8810	0·2811	1·3502
	062	Other textile products	1·30	0·0682	1·3166	0·9748	0·1752	1·3344
	063	Footwear	1·07	0·0695	1·0840	0·9890	0·2168	1·1252

Table 21. (contd.)

Code number, 33-sector breakdown	Code number, 194-sector breakdown	Sector	Parameter[1]					
			$(1 + t)$	W	A	$(1 - t)$	r	C
	064	Ready-made clothing	1·11	0·0695	1·1245	0·9890	0·2168	1·1587
	133	Jewellery, silverware and plated ware	3·52	0·0460	3·5504	0·9664	0·1696	2·7839
	134	Musical instruments	2·80	0·0460	2·8241	0·9664	0·1696	2·3969
	135	Fabricated plastic products	1·74	0·0460	1·7550	0·9664	0·1696	1·6937
	110	Cutlery, hand-tools and general hardware	1·45	0·0700	1·4691	0·9788	0·1367	1·4626
	125	Other electrical apparatus, equipment and appliances	2·25	0·0683	2·2790	0·9838	0·1935	1·9989
	130	Bicycles and motocycles	1·31	0·0736	1·3282	0·9861	0·1183	1·3346
	131	Other transport equipment	1·54	0·0736	1·5613	0·9861	0·1183	1·5347
	132	Photographic, optical and ophthalmic goods	1·98	0·0460	1·9970	0·9664	0·1696	1·8692
19	Modern	intermediate goods	1·17	0·0635	1·18	0·929	0·16	1·28
	043	Flour and other grain mill products	1·15	0·0768	1·1666	0·9872	0·1683	1·1923
	050	Animal feeds	1·05	0·0768	1·0652	0·9872	0·1683	1·1040
	061	Cordage, twine and net	0·92	0·0682	0·9318	0·9748	0·1752	0·9984
	068	Sawmill and planing mill products	0·92	0·0648	0·9313	0·9826	0·1644	0·9874
	070	Mill work products	1·15	0·0648	1·1640	0·9826	0·1644	1·1953
	071	Wooden containers	1·22	0·0648	1·2349	0·9826	0·1644	1·2561
	076	Pulp, paper, paperboard	1·31	0·0634	1·3257	0·9850	0·1750	1·3280
	077	Paper products	1·09	0·0634	1·1030	0·9850	0·1750	1·1405
	078	Paperboard products	1·09	0·0634	1·1030	0·9850	0·1750	1·1405
	082	Commercial printing	1·30	0·0464	1·3113	0·9735	0·1265	1·3360
	084	Tanned or finished leather	2·05	0·0697	2·0769	0·9791	0·1944	1·8713
	087	Tyres and inner tubes	1·51	0·0606	1·5272	0·9739	1·1414	1·5165
	089	Other rubber products	1·10	0·0606	1·1125	0·9739	0·1414	1·1579
	090	Basic industrial chemicals	1·18	0·0672	1·1949	0·9905	0·1991	1·2134
	092	Paints, varnishes and related compounds	1·11	0·0672	1·1240	0·9905	0·1991	1·1549
	096	Fertiliser	1·16	0·0672	1·1747	0·9905	0·1991	1·1969
	098	Other chemical products	1·24	0·0672	1·2556	0·9905	0·1991	1·2626
	099	Products of petroleum and coal	1·13	0·0652	1·1438	0·8250	0·1852	1·3968
	100	Hydraulic cement	1·25	0·0535	1·2625	0·9766	0·1519	1·2877
	101	Structural concrete products	1·07	0·0535	1·0808	0·9766	0·1519	1·1275
	102	Structural clay products	1·19	0·0535	1·2019	0·9766	0·1519	1·2352
	103	Glass and glass products	1·45	0·0535	1·4646	0·9766	0·1519	1·4575
	106	Blast and electric furnace and rolling mill products	1·29	0·0689	1·3067	0·9772	0·1385	1·3259

(*table continued overleaf*)

Table 21. (contd.)

Code number, 33-sector breakdown	Code number, 194-sector breakdown	Sector	Parameter[1]					
			$(1+t)$	W	A	$(1-t)$	r	C
	107	Iron and steel foundry products	1·10	0·0689	1·1142	0·9772	0·1385	1·1554
	111	Fabricated structural metal products	1·81	0·0700	1·8339	0·9788	0·1367	1·7562
	113	Fabricated wire products	1·29	0·0700	1·3070	0·9788	0·1367	1·3243
	115	Other fabricated metal products	1·40	0·0700	1·4185	0·9788	0·1367	1·4198
	123	Electric lamps and bulbs	2·25	0·0683	2·2790	0·9838	0·1935	1·9889
	128	Motor vehicle parts and supplies	1·18	0·0736	1·1963	0·9861	0·1183	1·2173
20		*Modern capital goods*	*1·23*	*0·0722*	*1·25*	*0·979*	*0·19*	*1·27*
	074	Metal furniture and fixtures	2·04	0·0588	2·0625	0·9570	0·1487	1·9581
	075	Other furniture and fixtures	0·92	0·0588	0·9302	0·9570	0·1487	1·0086
	112	Stamped, coated and engraved metals	1·12	0·0700	1·1348	0·9788	0·1367	1·1719
	116	Tractors and farm machinery	1·15	0·0442	1·1595	0·9860	0·2245	1·1915
	117	Industrial machinery	1·15	0·0442	1·1595	0·9860	0·2245	1·1915
	119	Other machinery, except electrical	1·41	0·0442	1·4217	0·9860	0·2245	1·3933
	120	Electrical industrial apparatus	1·20	0·0683	1·2654	0·9838	0·1935	1·2384
	122	Batteries	1·50	0·0683	1·5193	0·9838	0·1935	1·4773
	127	Motor vehicles	1·29	0·0736	1·3071	0·9861	0·1183	1·3160
21		*Export-oriented manufactured goods*	*1·04*	*0·0613*	*1·05*	*0·979*	*0·16*	*1·098*
	038	Canned fruits and fruit juices	0·92	0·0768	0·9333	0·9872	0·1683	0·9856
	045	Milled and refined sugar	1·35	0·0768	1·3695	0·9872	0·1683	1·3615
	048	Dessicated coconut products	0·92	0·0768	0·9333	0·9872	0·1683	0·9856
	069	Plywood and veneer	0·92	0·0648	0·9313	0·9826	0·1644	0·9874
	091	Vegetable and animal oils and fats	1·08	0·0672	1·0936	0·9905	0·1991	1·1684

II. Non-traded goods

22		*Construction*	*1·38*					
23		*Public utilities*	*1·68*			*0·935*	*0*	*1·39*
24		*Wholesale trade*	*1·23*					
25		*Retail trade*	*1·23*					
26		*Finance*	*1·23*					
27		*Rents*	*1·52*			*0·957*	*0*	*1·59*
28		*Modern transportation and communication*	*1·87*			*0·961*	*0*	*1·88*
29		*Traditional transportation*	*1·996*					

Table 21. (concl.)

Code number, 33-sector breakdown	Code number, 194-sector breakdown	Sector	Parameter[1]					
			$(1 + t)$	W	A	$(1 - t)$	r	C
30		Government			1·25			
31		Modern services			1·60	0·992	0·029	1·60
32		Traditional services			1·16	0·986	0·032	1·18

[1] Key:

$(1 + t)$	= realised nominal protection		$(1 - t)$	= net of tax price as percentage of market price
W	= wholesale margin as percentage of market price		r	= retail margin as percentage of market price
A_w	= accounting ratio for wholesale trade = 1·228		A_r	= accounting ratio for retail trade = 1·23
A	= accounting ratio derived from		C	= accounting ratio derived from

$$A = A_w(1 + t)/(A_w(1 - W) + W).$$

$$C = 1/(1 - t) \times \left(\frac{1 - r}{A} + \frac{r}{A_r} \right).$$

sectors 1–21 were revalued in terms of their tradeable value by using the 1965 data on nominal effective rates of protection given by Power and Sicat,[1] together with estimates derived from the National Economic Council's 194-sector table on the trade margins on the producer prices of these tradeable goods. Table 21 lists the nominal effective rates of protection and trade margins used,[2] and also gives the accounting ratios derived for the more important components of the composite tradeable categories in the 33-sector input-output table (i.e. modern consumer goods, modern intermediate goods, modern capital goods and export-oriented manufactured goods). These accounting ratios were derived by taking the value of each of the items within a category from the 194-sector table, and converting each of these items by the accounting ratio for that item. The accounting ratio for the composite sector is thus a weighted average of the accounting ratio for the items of which it is composed, the weights being the value of each of these items in the 194-sector table. The use of the accounting ratios for composite tradeable commodities can be a useful short cut in determining the accounting value of some trade-able items for which direct information on the ratio of its market to its border price is not available.

All the values hitherto determined are at producer prices. Hence these accounting ratios are strictly applicable only when converting the prices paid by producers for these items into their respective accounting prices. Consumers will in general face different

---

[1] J. H. Power and G. P. Sicat: *The Philippines: Industrialization and trade policies* (London, Oxford University Press, 1971), pp. 95–97.

[2] The margins we have taken are based on the data given in the 194-sector input-output table. However, it should be noted that the resulting margins are inconsistent with, and significantly lower than, those given in the *Survey of importers of durable equipment* (National Economic Council, Offices of Statistical Co-ordination and Standards, 1967). This survey (p. 26) found that the average trade mark-up on imported durable equipment was 52·9 per cent and reached colossal proportions in some cases (e.g. electrical household appliances, 178·7 per cent; gypsum plaster products, 160·6 per cent; industrial rubber belting, 113·1 per cent; agricultural machinery, 68·6 per cent). The obvious explanation that these margins reflect the monopoly profits of those lucky enough to receive import quotas for these items is not plausible, because the survey was carried out in 1964 when (in principle) there were no longer any quota restrictions on foreign trade. In the circumstances it is difficult to believe that the wholesale import trade is so uncompetitive that such large trade margins can be charged. We have therefore used the lower (and, it appears to us, more plausible) trade margins given in the 194-sector input–output table. However, this is clearly an area where further research would be very valuable.

Table 22. Non-traded good industries and their inputs

Code no.	Item	Sector										
		Construction	Public utilities	Wholesale trade	Retail trade	Finance	Rents	Modern transportation and communication	Traditional transportation	Government	Modern services	Traditional services
		22	23	24	25	26	27	28	29	30	31	32
Sector												
22	Construction	1·000	−0·002	−0·001	−0·001	−0·001	−0·018	−0·001	−0·002	0·0	−0·001	−0·001
23	Public utilities	−0·002	1·000	−0·004	−0·010	−0·005	−0·005	−0·005	−0·002	0·0	−0·008	−0·012
24	Wholesale trade	−0·067	−0·030	1·000	−0·005	−0·004	−0·005	−0·035	−0·017	0·0	−0·010	−0·035
25	Retail trade	−0·021	−0·023	−0·002	1·000	−0·003	−0·002	−0·024	−0·014	0·0	−0·014	−0·043
26	Finance	−0·009	−0·014	−0·018	−0·016	1·000	−0·014	−0·018	−0·001	0·0	−0·010	−0·009
27	Rents	−0·004	−0·008	−0·051	−0·073	−0·034	1·000	−0·012	−0·004	0·0	−0·018	−0·023
28	Modern transportation and communication	−0·014	−0·022	−0·031	−0·018	−0·013	−0·002	1·000	−0·009	0·02	−0·016	−0·010
29	Traditional transportation	0·0	0·0	0·0	0·0	0·0	0·0	0·0	1·000	0·0	0·0	0·0
30	Government	0·0	0·0	−0·001	−0·001	−0·002	0·0	−0·001	−0·001	1·000	−0·001	0·0
31	Modern services	−0·032	−0·029	−0·059	−0·042	−0·080	−0·018	−0·030	−0·002	0·0	1·000	−0·031
32	Traditional services	−0·008	−0·007	−0·012	−0·007	−0·008	−0·001	−0·012	0·0	0·0	−0·011	1·000

The B matrix: primary inputs

B1 Wages and salaries	−0·242	−0·225	−0·344	−0·344	−0·274	−0·204	−0·108	−0·112	−0·995	−0·342	−0·284
2 Capital consumption	−0·022	−0·093	−0·024	−0·025	−0·026	−0·094	−0·070	−0·022	0·000	−0·033	−0·014
3 Other value added	−0·187	−0·233	−0·403	−0·402	−0·469	−0·555	−0·190	−0·666	0·000	−0·321	−0·204
4 Tradeable	−0·312	−0·155	−0·017	−0·022	−0·020	−0·025	−0·186	−0·105	−0·001	−0·100	−0·288
5 Residual	−0·080	−0·159	−0·033	−0·034	−0·061	−0·057	−0·308	−0·043	+0·016	−0·115	−0·046
Total (A + B)	0·000	0·000	0·000	0·000	0·000	0·000	0·000	0·000	0·000	0·000	0·000

The C matrix: direct and indirect primary inputs

C1 Wages and salaries	0·304	0·290	0·400	0·395	0·331	0·227	0·168	0·130	0·996	0·406	0·343
2 Capital consumption	0·029	0·107	0·035	0·037	0·035	0·097	0·081	0·025	0·000	0·042	0·023
3 Other value added	0·260	0·311	0·483	0·483	0·539	0·583	0·267	0·688	0·001	0·395	0·280
4 Tradeable	0·330	0·180	0·038	0·038	0·038	0·035	0·210	0·110	0·002	0·120	0·301
5 Residual	0·077	0·112	0·044	0·047	0·057	0·058	0·274	0·047	0·001	0·037	0·053
Total	1·000	1·000	1·000	1·000	1·000	1·000	1·000	1·000	1·000	1·000	1·000

prices from producers, owing to the existence of retail trade margins and excise taxes on the commodities. In determining the accounting prices for commodities purchased by consumers, we have to add the border price equivalent value of the retail trade margin to the accounting producer price. The excise taxes are a transfer payment and thus do not represent any real domestic resource costs. The retail margins and net indirect taxes on the various commodities are given in table 21, together with the resulting accounting ratios for final consumer good prices of the products.

Non-traded goods

Having revalued the tradeable inputs at producer prices into the 11 non-traded good sectors, we are left with an 11 × 11 matrix of non-traded good inputs into the non-traded goods sectors (the non-traded good element represented by the trade margin in the wholesale price of the tradeable goods having been separated and amalgamated with the other direct trade margins for that sector). Call this the A matrix, whose elements a_{ij} are the direct inputs of non-traded good i per unit output of non-traded good j. We also have an 11 × 4 matrix of inputs of primary factors, one of which is now the tradeable cost of the traded goods used in the production of the sector. This is labelled the B matrix, and its elements b_{pj} give the direct primary input of b into non-traded good j.

The A matrix is first normalised, so that $a_{ii} = 1$, for all i, and then inverted. The inverse of the A matrix A^{-1} will have as its elements $\bar{a}_{ij}$, the *direct plus all indirect* inputs of non-traded good i, per unit of non-traded good j.

The total *direct and indirect primary* inputs in non-traded good j will then be given by post-multiplying the B matrix by the inverse of the A matrix to give a C matrix whose elements

$$\bar{c}_{pj} = \sum_i (b_{pj} \cdot \bar{a}_{ij}).$$

The A, B and C matrices derived from the 33-sector input–output table are given in table 22.

Next, we have to revalue the primary inputs in terms of our numeraire, aggregate savings expressed in foreign exchange. This was done as follows.

Tradeable. This is in foreign exchange equivalent value, and hence is socially valuable at par.

Wages and salaries. As a first approximation the shadow wage rate (SWR) for all the non-traded good industries was taken as 0·8 of the market wage. Strictly, the value of the SWRs and the accounting ratios which enter the SWR determination, through the revaluation of the output forgone or increased consumption components of the SWR, should be determined simultaneously.

Capital consumption. This was valued at border prices by applying the accounting ratio for modern capital goods (table 21).

Residual. This represents "taxes" which are not a social cost and hence are ignored.

Other value added. This comprises profits plus the earnings of self-employed workers in the various industries. We assume that the earnings of self-employed workers represent returns to entrepreneurial and managerial skills, and are valuable at par. For profits we assume (lacking any relevant data) that one-third is consumed by "capitalists", and as we do not put any social value on capitalist consumption (see the section on "Distributional weighting" below), are a cost at par; a further third is taxed away, and does not represent a social cost; and a final third is saved, which (again in terms of our numeraire) does not represent a social cost. The final accounting value of other value added then will be $E + V/3$, where E is the earnings of the self-employed and V is the market value of other value added.

Table 23.   Estimates of earnings from self-employment in non-traded good industries

Sector	n_i	w_i	m_i	W_i/V_i	E_i
Construction	0·084	51[1]	130[1]	0·294	0·068
Public utilities	0·000	68	130	0·284	0·000
Wholesale trade	0·743	66	90	0·399	0·401
Retail trade	0·743	66	90	0·394	0·401
Finance	0·743	69	130	0·329	0·461
Rents	0·743	58	90	0·226	0·261
Modern transportation and communication	0·214	81	130	0·162	0·063
Traditional transportation	0·313	61	90	0·127	0·059
Government	0·000	88	130	0·996	0·000
Modern services	0·045	102	130	0·402	0·023
Traditional services	0·482	40	66	0·337	0·268

Key:
n_i = percentage of self-employed in the total labour force in industry i (source: Bureau of the Census and Statistics: *Labour force survey*, Mar. 1971, table 2);
w_i = average earnings per week of all wage and salary earners in industry i (source: derived from ibid., table 49);
m_i = average earnings per week of self-employed in industry i (source: derived from ibid., table 47);
W_i/V_i = share of wages and salaries in value added industry i; and
E_i = share of earnings from self-employment in industry i (derived as described in text).

[1] The earnings figures taken were based on judgements about the likely groups within each sector whose average earnings would best correspond to the figures we seek.

How is E to be determined? Suppose that

n_i = percentage of self-employed in the total labour force in the non-traded good industry i;
w_i = average earnings per week of all wage and salary earners in industry i;
m_i = average earnings per week of self-employed in industry i;
W_i/V_i = share of wages and salaries in value added industry i; and
N_i = total labour force comprising both wage earners and self-employed in industry i.

Then E_i (the total earnings of the self-employed as a percentage of value added in industry i) is given by

$$E_i = \frac{n_i m_i N_i}{V_i} . \tag{1}$$

As $W_i = w_i N_i$

$$W_i/V_i = w_i N_i/V_i. \tag{2}$$

Hence, substituting the value of N_i/V_i from equation (2) into equation (1) we get

$$E_i = n_i m_i W_i/V_i \cdot 1/w_i. \tag{3}$$

Table 23 gives the data on n_i, m_i, w_i and W_i/V_i, used to estimate E_i in each non-traded good industry.

Data on n_i, w_i and m_i were derived from the Bureau of the Census and Statistics' *Labour Force Survey* for March 1971. W_i/V_i is given for each industry in the C matrix of table 22. The computed value of E_i is shown in the last column of table 23.

The above accounting values for each primary input of each non-traded good industry are then summed (see table 24) to derive the percentage of the unit cost at accounting prices. The inverse of these percentages is the accounting ratio at producer prices for the non-traded goods; these ratios are summarised in table 25. This table also gives the accounting ratios for these goods at consumer prices.

Table 24. Derivation of accounting values of direct and indirect primary inputs in non-traded goods

Code no.	Sector	M or S	Wages and salaries	Consump-tion	Profits	Tradeable	SUM ΣM ΣS	R 1 − ΣM / 1 − ΣS
22	Construction	M	0·3037	0·0289	0·2599	0·3302	0·9227	0·0773
		S	0·2430	0·0214	0·1321	0·3302	0·7267	0·2733
23	Public utilities	M	0·2899	0·1066	0·3105	0·1799	0·8869	0·1131
		S	0·2319	0·0790	0·1035	0·1799	0·5943	0·4057
24	Wholesale trade	M	0·4002	0·0352	0·4825	0·0381	0·9560	0·0440
		S	0·3202	0·0277	0·4284	0·0381	0·8144	0·1856
25	Retail trade	M	0·3955	0·0369	0·4833	0·0383	0·9540	0·0460
		S	0·3164	0·0291	0·4286	0·0383	0·8124	0·1876
26	Finance	M	0·3306	0·0353	0·5393	0·0382	0·9434	0·0566
		S	0·2645	0·0261	0·4872	0·0382	0·8160	0·1840
27	Rents	M	0·2271	0·0973	0·5831	0·0353	0·9428	0·0572
		S	0·1817	0·0721	0·3683	0·0353	0·6574	0·3426
28	Modern transportation and communication	M	0·1685	0·0809	0·2668	0·2096	0·7258	0·2742
		S	0·1348	0·0599	0·1312	0·2096	0·5355	0·4645
29	Traditional transportation	M	0·1304	0·0250	0·6883	0·1096	0·9533	0·0467
		S	0·1043	0·0185	0·2686	0·1096	0·5010	0·4990
30	Government	M	0·9960	0·0002	0·0010	0·0017	0·9989	0·0011
		S	0·7968	0·0001	0·0003	0·0017	0·7989	0·2011
31	Modern services	M	0·4059	0·0424	0·3951	0·1203	0·9637	0·0363
		S	0·3247	0·0314	0·1471	0·1203	0·6235	0·3765
32	Traditional services	M	0·3432	0·0232	0·2803	0·3015	0·9482	0·0518
		S	0·2746	0·0172	0·2720	0·3015	0·8653	0·1347

Key:

M = values at market prices;
S = values at accounting prices; and
R = residual.

Note: The M values are derived from the 1965 input–output table of the National Economic Council; the S values have been computed on the lines described in the text.

Table 25. Accounting ratios for non-traded goods

Code no.	Sector	Producer prices (A)	Consumer prices (C)
22	Construction	1·376	—
23	Public utilities	1·683	1·39
24	Wholesale trade	1·228	—
25	Retail trade	1·231	—
26	Finance	1·226	—
27	Rents	1·521	1·59
28	Modern transportation and communication	1·867	1·88
29	Traditional transportation	1·996	—
30	Government	1·252	—
31	Modern services	1·604	1·60
32	Traditional services	1·156	1·18

Table 25 can now be used directly to revalue any non-traded good used in production or consumption. The market price is simply divided by the accounting ratio given for it, at producer (consumer) prices if it is to be used in production (consumption).

It should, however, be noted that all the accounting ratios for these non-agricultural commodities are based on 1965 data, since the input–output tables themselves were based on data for that year, as were the rates of effective nominal protection given in Power and Sicat.[1] However, there is some reason to believe that these accounting ratios have not altered significantly since then,[2] for the Philippine economy at the moment (1973) seems to be adjusting to the devaluation of 1969, which appears to have been excessive. The 1969 balance-of-payments crisis was essentially caused by a high level of election spending. The "correct" cure would have been a reduction in excess demand.[3] The substantial devaluation, which moreover was not accompanied by any trade liberalisation, led to rapid inflation (see figures 14 and 15)—more specifically, a profit inflation, which resulted in a fall in real wages.

This devaluation-cum-inflation-induced shift in income distribution towards those with high savings propensities should have resulted in a reduction in excess demand and hence an improvement in the balance of payments. However, if this analysis is correct, this implies that, given the unchanging level of import restrictions (pre- and post-devaluation), devaluation was not the appropriate instrument for correcting the balance-of-payments deficit, for the latter was not primarily caused by a disequilibrium between the prices of traded and non-traded goods[4] but rather by excess aggregate demand. Devaluation could cure the latter by an inflation-induced shift in the distribution of income; but if the relative prices of traded and non-traded goods were initially close to an "equilibrium" level (with given and unchanged trade restrictions), the same relative price ratio would again be restored following devaluation, but at a higher absolute level of the prices of both traded and non-traded goods.

Figure 15, which charts movements in the wholesale price index of domestic and imported products, seems partly to confirm this analysis. After 1966 the prices of non-traded goods rose more rapidly than import prices, and hence the relative price of non-traded and traded goods may have risen above its equilibrium level. This would have implied a small balance-of-payments deficit, for which a small devaluation in 1969 would have sufficed. That the 1969 devaluation was too great is borne out both by the rapid increase since 1969 in the indices for traded and non-traded (domestic) goods and by the fairly close correspondence between their levels; this implies that the 1966 relative price ratio between the two had been restored, but that the absolute price level had also risen markedly.

Thus we may conclude that the accounting price ratios we have calculated on the basis of 1965 relative price data are probably not too inaccurate indicators of *relative* accounting prices at present (1973). Clearly, however, if trade liberalisation is undertaken in the future, it will be necessary to recompute these ratios for the new equilibrium relative price of traded and non-traded goods which would then be established.

---

[1] Power and Sicat: *The Philippines*, op. cit.

[2] It may also be noted that our methodology does not imply that we have derived "free trade" accounting ratios. See Lal: "Adjustments for trade distortions . . .", op. cit.

[3] See H. G. Johnson: "The balance of payments" in his *Money, trade and economic growth* (London, George Allen and Unwin; Cambridge, Mass., Harvard University Press, 2nd ed., 1967).

[4] See Lal: "Adjustments for trade distortions . . .", op. cit., for an analysis of the way in which exchange rate changes could affect the relative price of traded and non-traded goods, and hence relative accounting prices.

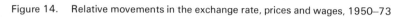

Figure 14.   Relative movements in the exchange rate, prices and wages, 1950–73

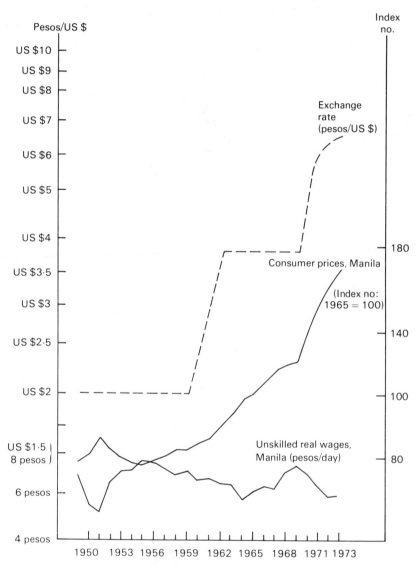

Figure 15.   Price series, 1950–73 (1965 = 100)

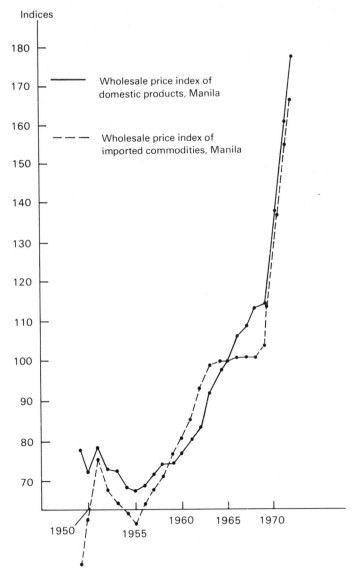

Indices

Table 26. Domestic and "world" prices of rice, 1960–72

Year	Unit import value	World average export unit value	$(1) \div (2)$	Average wholesale price, Manila	$(4) \div (1)$	$(4) \div (2)$
	(1)	(2)	(3)	(4)	(5)	(6)
1960	145·9	103·3	1·41	204·56	1·40	1·98
1961	114·2	109·5	1·04	240·98	2·11	2·11
1962	—[1]	122·0		245·81	·	2·02
1963	108·46	121·7	0·89	133·75	1·23	1·10
1964	110·42	124·8	0·89	163·37	1·48	1·31
1965	119·75	127·5	0·94	154·35	1·29	1·21
1966	133·0	140·2	0·95	176·78	1·33	1·26
1967	149·72	163·6	0·92	194·41	1·30	1·19
1968	—[1]	180·6	·	179·53	·	0·99
1969	—[1]	165·4	·	181·00	·	1·09
1970	—[1]	136·4	·	120·34	·	0·88
1971	83·93	129·0	0·65	149·55	1·78	1·16
1972	88·00	·	·	167·88	1·91	·
Average	117·04	135·33	0·96 $(0·86)^2$	177·87	1·54 $(1·52)^2$	1·36 $(1·32)^2$

[1] There were no imports in the years which are indicated by a dash.   [2] The figures in brackets have been derived by taking averages of the "average" figures.

Source: (1) Central Bank; (2) FAO: *FAO Commodity Review and Outlook, 1971–1972* (Rome, 1972), and information supplied by FAO.

RICE AND PALAY

In this section we make estimates for one of the more important agricultural commodities, i.e. rice. The accounting price of rice will be important in revaluing the food basket of consumers at accounting prices, whilst that of palay (rough rice) will be of use in determining the accounting value of output forgone by employing agricultural workers. Similar accounting ratios should also be derived for maize[1] and coconuts, but because of lack of time and data we have not made the calculations for these other agricultural commodities. We shall therefore be assuming that the accounting ratios we derive for rice and palay will also be approximately correct for other agricultural products, on the assumption that these other products will be substitutable at the margin in production or consumption with palay or rice. Whilst this assumption may not be unreasonable for maize, it is probably not a very good one for coconuts; hence, even though coconuts are not of importance for this study, a separate accounting price for them should be derived.

Rice

Table 26 gives the unit import value, the average wholesale Manila price, and the world average export unit values of rice between 1960 and 1972. The movements in the three series are also charted in figures 16 and 17 (in terms of pesos per metric ton and

[1] i.e. "Indian corn" (in US usage = "corn").

Figure 16.   The price of rice, 1960–72
              (pesos per metric ton)

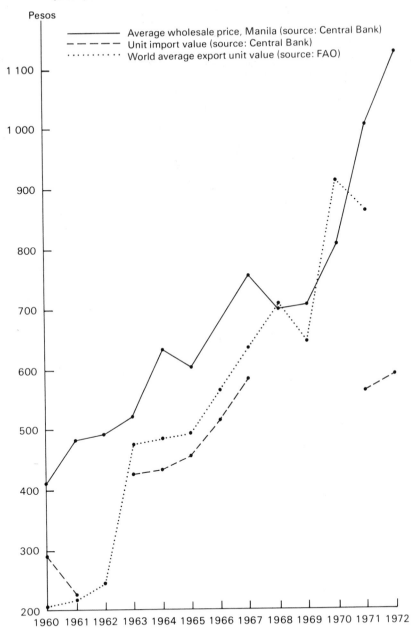

Figure 17.   The price of rice, 1960–72
(US$ per metric ton)

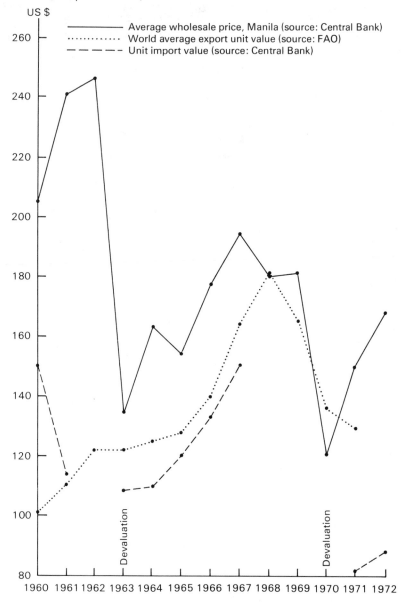

US$ per metric ton). From these it appears that the price differential between the unit import value and the Manila wholesale price has ranged from 23 per cent in 1963 to 111 per cent in 1961. The reason for this seems to be the role that rice imports play in the economy of the Philippines.[1] Mangahas and Librero[2] have noted that the Government has been the sole importer or exporter of rice, and hence the volume of rice imports/exports has depended upon the Government's assessment of the predicted balance between domestic production and the demand for rice in each year. They also note that predicted rice "shortages" (and hence the actual imports of rice allowed) have coincided with election years. As rice is an important part of the food basket of the urban poor, the ruling party has sought to improve its electoral chances by keeping urban rice prices low in election years.

This has meant that, as the domestic price of rice is determined by the aggregate supply and demand in any year, the actual price established is very sensitive to the annual quantity of rice imports and hence to the estimated rice "shortage". As the absolute size of the difference between estimated demand and domestic supply in any year has been between 5 and 10 per cent,[3] the estimate of the rice "shortage" is very sensitive to errors of estimation in either rice production or rice requirements. As Mangahas says, "It would be very easy to mistake a condition of shortage for a condition of surplus and vice versa. . . . It seems possible that there was a surplus mistaken for a shortage in 1967."[4] Therefore, given the political cycle in rice imports,[5] the behaviour of the domestic rice price and hence its differential with the "border" price is likely to be unpredictable. This means that using an average accounting ratio for any period for converting wholesale rice prices into their border price equivalents will be treacherous. It will therefore be necessary to derive the accounting ratios for each of the years in the past. To do this we need to mark up the unit import value for port handling, brokerage fees, internal transport and wholesale costs. We assume that the wholesale margin is about 8·5 per cent. This can be derived from the data in the 194-sector input–output table. Lacking any data on port handling and internal transport costs, we have arbitrarily assumed that port handling costs are about 10 per cent and that transport costs are about 9 per cent of the c.i.f. price. The border price of rice will then be:

$$P_{cif} (1 + 0·1/A_h) \times (1 + 0·09/A_t) \times (1 + 0·085/A_w)$$

where

P_{cif} = import price;
A_h = accounting ratio for port handling, which is taken to be "modern services";
A_t = accounting ratio for modern transportation; and
A_w = accounting ratio for wholesale trade.

The values of the above accounting ratios from table 25 are: $A_h = 1·60$; $A_t = 1·87$; and $A_w = 1·23$. Hence the border price of rice will be

$$P_{cif} \, 1·06 \times 1·05 \times 1·07 = 1·19 P_{cif}.$$

---

[1] From the data it also appears that the Government has succeeded in getting a price for imported rice better than the average world export prices.

[2] M. Mangahas and A. R. Librero: *The high-yielding varieties of rice in the Philippines: A perspective*, Discussion paper no. 73-11, 15 June 1973 (Manila, University of the Philippines, School of Economics, Institute of Economic Development and Research).

[3] M. Mangahas: "Efficient forecasting and Philippine rice import/export policy", in Mangahas and Librero, op. cit.

[4] Mangahas and Librero, op. cit., pp. 11–12. From figures 16 and 17 it can be seen that whilst the world average export unit value of rice was rising the average wholesale price in Manila was falling.

[5] Thus the Government announced large rice imports in July 1973, just before the referendum at the end of the month.

Men or machines

Table 27. Derivation of the accounting ratio for the wholesale price of rice in Manila (A_R^M), 1960–67, 1971–72
(pesos per metric ton)

Year	Wholesale price, Manila (P_d)	Import price (P_{cif})	Accounting price of wholesale rice $(P_{cif}(1 \cdot 19))$	Accounting ratio (A_R^M)
	(1)	(2)	(3)	(4)
1960	409·11	291·8	347·242	1·178
1961	481·96	228·4	271·800	1·773
1962	491·61	—	—	—
1963	521·61	422·99	503·358	1·036
1964	637·14	430·64	512·461	1·243
1965	601·96	467·03	555·77	1·083
1966	689·46	518·70	617·25	1·117
1967	758·21	583·91	694·85	1·091
1971	1 013·93	569·05	677·16	1·497
1972	1 138·21	596·64	710·00	1·603

Note: $A_R^M = P_d/[P_{cif}(1 \cdot 19)]$. See text for derivation.

Table 28. Average prices received by farmers for palay, 1960–72
(pesos per metric ton)

Year	Price received by farmers for palay	Wholesale price of rice, Manila	Ratio $(2) \div (1)$ (P_p^a)	Computed border price of palay	Ratio of border price to price received by farmers $(4) \div (1)$
	(1)	(2)	(3)	(4)	(5)
1960	209·55	409·11	1·952	243·07	1·160
1961	245·91	481·96	1·959	183·26	0·745
1962	234·32	491·61	2·098	—	—
1963	284·77	521·61	1·832	352·35	1·237
1964	328·86	637·14	1·937	358·72	1·091
1965	333·86	601·96	1·803	389·00	1·165
1966	370·23	689·46	1·862	432·08	1·167
1967	378·18	758·21	2·005	486·40	1·286
1968	360·23	700·18	1·944		
1969	372·27	705·89	1·894		
1970	412·23	815·89	1·979		
1971	(524·54)[1]	1 013·93		474·01	(0·904)[1]
1972	(588·83)[1]	1 138·21		497·00	(0·844)[1]
		Average	1·933		1·067

Hence the average accounting ratio for palay $(A_p = P_p^m/P_p^a)$ is then $1/1 \cdot 067 = 0 \cdot 937$.

[1] The figures in brackets in cols. (1) and (5) have been derived by assuming that the prices received by farmers for palay in 1971 would have had the same ratio to the Manila wholesale price as the average for this ratio given in col. (3).

Source: Col. (1) Department of Agriculture and Natural Resources, Bureau of Agricultural Economics: *Handbook of Philippine agricultural and natural resources, 1971*; col. (2) Central Bank; col. (4) computed by derivation given in the text. Border price of palay = 0·7 border price of rice in Manila, the latter values being given in col. (3) of table 27.

Table 29. Derivation of the accounting ratio for rice milling

Inputs		Values at market prices (pesos) (M)	Values at accounting prices (pesos) (A)
(1)	Palay	1 234 531	
(2)	Miscellaneous intermediate inputs	24 509	20 749·8
(3)	Trade	118 551	96 515·4
(4)	Rents	2 450	1 610·6
(5)	Transportation	10 750	5 590·0
(6)	Traditional services	13 601	11 764·9
(7)	Wages and salaries	86 669	69 335·2
(8)	Capital consumption	26 573	21 258·4
(9)	Profits	193 690	64 563·3
(10)	Taxes	11 466	—
		1 722 750	291 387·6 (Total less palay)

Notes: The accounting ratios used to determine the values at accounting prices were taken from table 21, namely for item (2) intermediate goods, 1·18; (3) trade, 1·23; (4) rents, 1·52; (5) approximate average for traditional and modern transportation, 1·92; (6) traditional services, 1·16; (7) 0·8 of the market wage; (8) modern capital goods, 1·25; (9) one-third of profits assumed taxed and one-third saved and not a social cost, one-third consumed and taken as a social cost; (10) transfer payment, hence no social cost.

Source: M from item 041 in the 194-sector input–output table.

The accounting ratio for milling costs (A_m), *exclusive* of the costs of palay, is $(1,722,750 - 1,234,531)/291,388 = 1·7$.

If the domestic wholesale price is P_d the accounting ratio for rice will be

$$A_R = P_d/1·19P_{cif}.$$

Table 27 derives the accounting ratio for the wholesale price of rice in Manila, using this derivation.

Palay

Table 28 gives data on the average prices received by palay farmers between 1960 and 1972, and their ratio to the average wholesale price of rice in Manila. It shows that the average price they receive is about 51·7 per cent of the Manila wholesale price ($1/1·933 = 0·517$). This differential can be accounted for by the costs of converting palay into rice (milling costs), transportation costs and the wholesale margin. This could be used as a crude way of deriving the border price of palay (P_p^a) which, given the border price of rice in the wholesale Manila market (P_r^a), would then be

$$P_p^a = 0·517P_r^a.$$

We can, however, improve on this by making use of the data for milled rice in the 194-sector input–output table. This has been aggregated into its main components and is given in table 29. The Manila wholesale price of rice will be made up of the costs of palay, milling costs, the wholesale margin and transport costs to Manila. We can therefore derive the border price of palay as follows: the Manila wholesale border price of rice (P_r^a) will be the sum of the border price of palay (P_p^a), the costs at border prices of rice milling (K_m^a), the wholesale trade margin on milled rice at border prices (W_m^a) and transport costs at border prices (T_m^a) for shipping the rice to Manila; hence

$$P_p^a = P_r^a - K_m^a - W_m^a - T_m^a.$$

Table 29 shows that milling costs other than those on account of palay are 40 per cent of the value of milled rice. We assume that, on average, transport costs of 10 per cent of the price of milled rice at the "factory gate" are incurred when shipping the milled rice to Manila. The wholesale margin is assumed, as before, to be 8·5 per cent. Furthermore, we need to make some assumptions about the quantity of palay required to yield a given quantity of milled rice. We can estimate the rough transformation ratio from the data given in table 29 on the total value of the outputs of milled rice and inputs of palay, together with the palay and Manila wholesale rice prices for 1965.

Thus the total value of milled rice in 1965, from table 29, was 1,722,750 pesos. To this we must add 10 per cent transportation costs and 8·43 per cent wholesale margin to derive a value of 2,054,776 pesos for the milled rice at the wholesale price obtaining in Manila. The latter, from table 28, was 601·96 pesos per metric ton in 1965, and hence the *quantity* of milled rice represented by the value given in table 29 will be 2,054,776/601·96 = 3,413·48 metric tons. The quantity of palay needed to produce this quantity of milled rice will then be the value of the palay output in table 29, namely 1,234,531 pesos divided by the 1965 palay price of 333·86 pesos per metric ton, which yields the quantity of palay as 1,234,531/333·86 = 3,697·75 metric tons. Therefore, to produce 1 metric ton of rice requires 3,413·48/3,697·75 = 1·08 metric tons of palay.

We can then construct the wholesale price of rice per metric ton in Manila, given a palay price of 100 per 1·08 metric tons, as follows:

Price of palay	100	per 1·08 metric tons of palay (or 92·59 per metric ton)
Milling costs	40	
Transport costs	14	
Wholesale margin	13	
Price of rice	167	per metric ton.

Thus, in reverse, if we know the price of rice in Manila, the price of palay per 1·08 metric tons can be derived as follows. The ratios of milling, transport and wholesale costs to the Manila wholesale costs can be applied to derive the value of these various costs at market prices, the latter being deflated by the relevant accounting ratio for rice milling, transport and wholesale trade to obtain their border price equivalents. Thus, for example, if the border price of wholesale rice in Manila is P_r^a, the wholesale margin at market prices will be $(13/167)P_r^a = 0.078P_r^a$ and at border prices will be $0.078P_r^a/A_w$ (where A_w is the accounting ratio for converting wholesale margin values from market into border prices). A similar argument applied to the other components making up the Manila wholesale price yields the border price of palay as

$$P_p^a = P_r^a \left(1 - \frac{0.078}{A_w} - \frac{0.084}{A_t} - \frac{0.24}{A_m} \right) \text{ per 1·08 metric tons of palay}$$

or

$$P_p^a = \frac{P_r^a}{1·08} \left(1 - \frac{0.078}{A_w} - \frac{0.084}{A_t} - \frac{0.24}{A_m} \right) \text{ per metric ton of palay.}$$

Table 30.   "Farm gate" prices for palay by region in selected years

Region[1]	Prices per metric ton (pesos)			Ratio of regional price to all-Philippines price			
	1965–66	1966–67	1971–72	1965–66	1966–67	1971–72	Average
	(1)	(2)	(3)	(4)	(5)	(6)	(7)
II	402·3	443·2	581·8	1·128	1·175	1·053	1·119
III	325·0	338·6	568·2	0·911	0·897	1·029	0·946
IV	388·6	425·0	627·3	1·089	1·126	1·136	1·117
V	356·8	379·6	529·6	1·000	1·006	0·959	0·988
VI	340·9	365·9	518·2	0·955	0·970	0·938	0·954
VII	338·6	372·7	559·1	0·949	0·988	1·012	0·983
VIII	363·6	365·9	554·6	1·019	0·970	1·004	0·998
IX	350·0	347·7	572·7	0·981	0·922	1·037	0·980
X	329·6	356·8	502·3	0·924	0·946	0·910	0·927
All Philippines	*356·8*	*377·3*	*552·3*	*1·000*	*1·000*	*1·000*	*1·000*

[1] For names of regions, see table 1B.

Source: Bureau of Agricultural Economics (BAECON)

The values of A_w and A_t from table 25 are 1·23 and 1·87 respectively and the value of A_m derived in table 29 is 1·7. This gives us the border price of palay as

$$P_p^a = 0·7 P_r^a.$$

From this the computed border prices of palay and their ratio to prices received by palay farmers between 1960 and 1972 are given in table 28.

These ratios are of some interest. They show that, on average, the imputed border price of palay has been about 7 per cent higher than the prices actually received by farmers. As by our method the imputed border price is set by the border price of rice, which on average has been lower than the domestic market price (see table 27), it is clear that most of the distortions between the border and market price of palay lie in processing the palay into rice and shipping it to Manila. What is more, as the imputed border price of palay is on average slightly higher than the price received by farmers, this implies that the "inefficiencies" in the processing, wholesaling and shipping sectors constitute a small indirect tax on the incomes of palay farmers who, in the absence of these distortions, would have received the higher imputed border price. Thus there may have been a small transfer of income from palay producers to the intermediaries involved in converting it into rice and bringing the rice into the shops in Manila. However, given the likelihood of errors in using the same conversion factors and accounting ratios for the components of the accounting prices of palay, and the accounting ratios for rice milling, too much should probably not be read into this divergence between the average imputed accounting and market prices for palay.

The border prices of palay that we calculated in table 28 are the average accounting prices for the whole of the Philippines. As table 30 shows, however, there are significant regional price variations in the prices of palay the farmers receive. It will therefore be necessary to determine regional accounting ratios, to convert the regional market prices (P_{pj}^m) received by farms into all-Philippines average border price of palay (P_p^a). Since we are measuring all our border values in terms of the all-Philippines average market price of palay, P_p^m will be

$$P_p^m = P_{pj}^m / r_j.$$

Table 31.   Accounting ratios for palay by region

Region[1]	r_j [2]	A_{pj} [3]
II	1·119	1·046
III	0·946	0·884
IV	1·117	1·044
V	0·988	0·923
VI	0·954	0·892
VII	0·983	0·919
VIII	0·998	0·933
IX	0·980	0·916
X	0·927	0·866

All Philippines $A_p = P_p^m / P_p^a = 0·937$

[1] For names of regions, see table 1B.   [2] From col. (7), table 30.   [3] $A_{pj} = r_j / 1·07$ (see text).

The relationship between P_p^m and the all-Philippines average border price of palay (P_p^a) from table 28 is

$$P_p^a = 1·07 P_p^m.$$

Hence

$$P_p^a = 1·07 P_{pj}^m / r_j$$

or

$$A_{pj} = P_{pj}^m / P_p^a = \frac{r_j}{1·07}.$$

The above relationship is used in table 31 to determine the regional accounting ratios for prices received by palay farmers. It should be noted that these accounting ratios convert the market price of palay in region j into the all-Philippines border price of palay. This table summarises all our accounting ratios for palay.

CONSUMPTION CONVERSION FACTORS

Part of the impact of the increased use on a project of a particular input (including labour) may be a change in the consumption of other goods and services in the economy. Thus let us suppose, for instance, that rice is demanded by the project and will in part be supplied to it by reductions in rice consumption elsewhere in the economy. This release of rice for the project must be the result of the bidding-up of the domestic rice price, which induces consumers to switch part of their expenditure on rice to other goods and services. The accounting cost of the rice which is now made available to the project will therefore be the accounting cost of the goods and services towards which consumer expenditure is switched. But it will not be possible, in most cases, to determine precisely the goods and services to which consumer expenditure switches. However, assuming that it switches to the average consumption bundle consumed in the economy, we can derive an aggregate consumption conversion factor as follows. We first obtain a breakdown of average consumer expenditure into its various components for the Philippines from the household income and expenditure survey. The values of these components (as well as those for total average expenditure) will obviously be at market prices. We next revalue each of these components at accounting prices, by dividing the market value of each item by its accounting ratio. The values at accounting prices are then summed, and the ratio of the

Table 32. Conversion factors for family expenditures by region

Item	All Philippines M²	T²	I M	T	II M	T	III M	T	IV M	T	V M	T	VI M	T	VII M	T	VIII M	T	IX M	T	X M	T
Food	53.7	48.82	41.5	37.73	53.4	41.08	50.6	41.08	55.5	57.71	52.6	42.69	54.3	48.26	55.4	51.71	59.0	51.30	59.2	53.64	56.7	55.59
Alcoholic beverages	1.7	1.21	0.8	0.57	1.8	1.28	1.5	1.28	0.9	0.64	1.4	1.00	1.9	1.9	2.8	2.8	2.7	1.99	3.2	1.92	1.9	1.35
Tobacco	3.3	1.90	2.8	1.61	2.6	1.50	3.2	1.50	3.6	1.84	3.4	2.07	3.3	3.2	3.2	1.90	2.8	1.84	3.2	1.61	6.2	2.36
Housing	9.4	5.91	18.0	11.32	9.8	6.16	7.5	6.16	7.7	4.72	3.6	4.84	10.0	6.29	7.1	6.29	6.9	4.47	6.3	4.34	6.2	3.90
Fuel, light and water	3.6	2.59	3.9	2.81	3.2	2.45	4.8	2.45	3.1	2.23	2.4	3.6	1.8	3.3	2.4	2.37	2.3	2.51	3.7	1.95	3.5	2.52
Household furnishings and equipment	2.3	1.95	2.1	1.78	1.6	2.71	1.6	2.71	1.7	1.44	2.5	2.59	1.8	1.8	1.5	1.53	2.5	2.03	2.6	2.12	3.2	1.61
Household operation	2.4	2.03	3.3	2.80	1.6	1.36	2.7	1.36	6.7	2.29	5.8	2.12	6.7	4.36	7.4	5.04	4.9	1.44	6.3	3.68	6.8	4.74
Clothing and other wear	6.2	4.66	5.9	4.44	6.2	4.66	4.1	4.66	3.08	1.19	1.8	4.36	1.5	1.5	1.5	1.5	1.2	5.56	1.6	6.3	1.4	6.8
Personal care	1.6	1.36	1.7	1.44	1.9	1.61	1.4	1.61	1.8	0.75	2.3	1.53	1.5	1.5	1.5	1.27	1.2	1.27	1.6	1.02	1.4	1.19
Medical care	1.8	1.13	1.9	1.19	1.8	1.13	1.2	1.13	1.7	1.01	3.5	1.44	2.4	2.4	1.6	1.50	2.5	1.00	1.6	1.00	1.6	1.00
Transportation and communication	2.9	1.54	4.5	2.39	1.5	1.44	1.9	1.44	1.8	0.68	1.8	1.86	1.8	1.8	1.7	0.96	1.4	1.49	1.9	1.33	2.0	1.06
Recreation	1.8	1.53	2.4	2.03	4.3	1.27	0.8	1.27	1.5	2.81	3.0	1.53	2.1	2.1	3.6	1.78	1.4	1.44	1.3	1.19	3.2	1.53
Education	3.7	2.31	4.7	2.94	0.7	2.69	4.5	2.69	2.8	0.25	0.8	1.88	3.8	3.8	0.6	2.25	2.7	2.25	1.69	0.5	2.00	3.2
Gifts and contributions	0.6	0.50	0.6	0.50	0.4	0.58	0.3	0.58	0.7	0.13	0.2	0.67	0.4	0.4	0.6	0.33	0.4	0.50	0.33	0.5	0.42	0.6
Taxes	0.3	0	0.9	0	0.6	0.40	0.1	0.40	0.3	0.20	0.4	0.26	0.6	0.6	0.2	0.40	0.2	0.46	0.33	0.5	0.33	1.1
Personal effects	0.6	0.40	0.7	0.46	0.6	0.46	0.2	0.13	0.3	1.09	0.4	1.59	0.6	0.50	0.7	0.50	1.1	1.17	0.9	0.92	1.5	0.75
Miscellaneous goods and services	1.5	1.25	2.5	2.09	2.1	1.75	1.3	1.75	1.2	2.10	1.9	1.00	2.0	1.90	1.4	1.90	2.4	1.76	2.18	2.04	0.75	2.04
Food and refreshments	2.0	1.82	1.4	1.27	1.7	1.31	2.2	1.31	2.6	0.07	2.3	2.11	2.3	2.0	2.4	0.21	0.5	0.21	0.36	0.4	0.28	0.3
Alcoholic beverages	0.3	0.21	0.2	0.14	0.2	0.14	0.1	0.14	0.2	0.14	0.2	0.14	0.3	0.3	0.3	0.21	0.5	0.21	0.06	0.1	0.06	0.3
Tobacco	0.1	0.06	0	0	0	0	0	0	0.2	0.12	0.1	0.06	0.1	0.1	0.1	0.06	0.1	0.06	0.06	0.2	0.12	0.2
Total	99.8	81.38	99.8	77.51	99.9	73.32	100.0	85.60	99.9	73.48	100.0	81.72	100.0	84.00	99.9	82.75	100.0	82.82	99.7	83.49	99.8	86.31
Conversion factor (M ÷ T)		1.23		1.29		1.36		1.17		1.36		1.22		1.19		1.21		1.21		1.19		1.16

¹ For names of regions, see table 1B. ² M = value at market prices; T = tradeable value.

Notes: *Food:* this item has been converted into its accounting values by using the accounting ratio for rice as follows. The accounting ratio for wholesale rice in Manila (*A*) in 1965, from table 27, was 1.083. This gives us the accounting price of rice in Manila at producer prices. To obtain the accounting ratio of consumer prices, we assume that the retail margin for rice (*r*) is 10 per cent. Then, given that the accounting ratio for retail trade from table 21 is 1.23 and that taxes are 0.007 of the retail market prices, we get the accounting ratio for retailed rice in Manila as $1/0.993$ $[(0.9/1.083) + (0.1/1.231)] = 1/0.9056 = 1.1$. This accounting ratio was used to correct the all-Philippines, urban and Region I market prices into accounting prices. The regional accounting prices were derived by assuming that the average difference between the regional and all-Philippines palay prices given in table 31 also applies to the inter-regional accounting prices of rice. Then the accounting ratios for the regions are: II, 1.3; III, 1.05:

IV, 1.3: V, 1.09: VI, 1.05: VII, 1.08: VIII, 1.1: IX, 1.08: X, 1.02. The rural market price of rice was converted into its accounting price as follows. The ratio of the average border price of palay to the prices received by farmers is 1.067 (from table 28). Assuming that the same ratio holds between the border price and the rural market price (paid by farmers) for rice, we have the accounting ratio for rural rice as $1/1.067 = 0.937$. *Other items:* the following accounting ratios for converting consumer market prices into accounting prices derived in tables 21, 22 and 25 were used: alcoholic beverages, 1.405: tobacco, 1.738: housing, 1.59: fuel, light and water, 1.39: household furnishings and equipment, 1.29: household operation, 1.29: clothing, 1.405: housing, 1.738: medical care, 1.59: transportation and communication, 1.6: transportation and communication, 1.198: gifts and contributions, 1.29: household operation, 1.88: recreation, 1.18: education, 1.6: gifts and contributions, 1.198: taxes, no social cost: personal effects, 1.51: miscellaneous goods and services, 1.198.

115

Table 33. Conversion factors for family expenditures by expenditure group

Item	Urban M¹	Urban T¹	(3 000–3 999 pesos) M	T	(4 000–4 999 pesos) M	T	(8 000–9 999 pesos) M	T	(10 000–14 000 pesos) M	T	Rural M	T	(2 500–2 999 pesos) M	T
Food	47.1	42.82	54.7	49.73	51.7	47.00	42.9	39.00	41.8	38.00	59.3	63.29	60.6	64.67
Alcoholic beverages	1.3	0.93	1.4	1.00	1.9	1.35	0.7	0.50	1.3	0.93	2.0	1.42	1.8	1.28
Tobacco	3.0	1.73	3.5	2.01	3.4	1.96	2.6	1.50	2.4	1.38	3.5	2.01	3.8	2.19
Housing	12.5	7.86	10.8	6.79	11.7	7.36	14.9	9.37	13.7	8.62	6.8	4.28	6.4	4.03
Fuel, light and water	3.6	2.59	3.8	2.73	3.4	2.45	3.5	2.52	3.4	2.45	3.6	2.59	3.8	2.73
Household furnishings and equipment	2.6	2.20	1.8	1.53	2.0	1.69	3.6	3.05	3.0	2.54	2.1	1.78	1.6	1.36
Household operation	3.0	2.54	2.1	1.78	2.6	2.20	3.0	2.97	3.9	3.31	1.9	1.61	1.6	1.36
Clothing and other wear	6.3	4.74	5.9	4.44	6.0	4.51	6.2	4.66	6.5	4.89	6.2	4.66	6.3	4.74
Personal care	1.8	1.53	1.8	1.53	1.8	1.53	1.9	1.61	2.0	1.69	1.4	1.19	1.3	1.10
Medical care	2.0	1.25	1.8	1.13	2.6	1.63	2.2	1.38	1.9	1.19	1.7	1.06	1.7	1.06
Transportation and communication	4.0	2.13	3.0	1.60	3.1	1.65	3.6	1.91	4.4	2.34	2.0	1.06	1.9	1.01
Recreation	2.2	1.86	1.5	1.27	1.8	1.53	3.3	2.80	2.2	1.86	1.5	1.27	1.4	1.19
Education	4.4	2.75	3.3	2.06	3.3	2.06	5.3	3.31	6.3	3.94	3.1	1.94	3.1	1.94
Gifts and contributions	0.7	0.58	0.4	0.33	0.4	0.33	0.7	0.58	0.9	0.75	0.5	0.42	0.5	0.42
Taxes	0.5	0	0.1	0	0.3	0	0.3	0	0.5	0	0.2	0	0.1	0
Personal effects	0.6	0.41	0.4	0.26	0.4	0.26	0.5	0.33	0.8	0.53	0.6	0.41	0.5	0.33
Miscellaneous goods and services	2.2	1.84	1.6	1.34	1.6	1.34	2.5	2.09	2.7	2.25	0.9	0.75	0.4	0.33
Food and refreshments	1.9	1.73	1.7	1.55	1.7	1.55	1.8	1.64	1.9	1.73	2.2	2.35	2.4	2.56
Alcoholic beverages	0.3	0.21	0.2	0.14	0.2	0.14	0.3	0.21	0.3	0.21	0.3	0.21	0.6	0.43
Tobacco	0.1	0.06	0.1	0.06	0.1	0.06	0.1	0.06	0.1	0.06	0.1	0.06	0.1	0.06
Total	100.0	79.96	99.9	81.28	100.0	80.60	99.9	79.49	100.0	78.67	99.9	92.36	99.9	92.79
Conversion Factor M ÷ T		1.25		1.23		1.24		1.26		1.27		1.08		1.08

¹ M = value at market prices; T = tradeable value.
Notes: The notes to table 32 apply to the present table also.

total average consumer expenditure at market to accounting prices is the aggregate consumption conversion factor for the Philippines.

This average, however, will conceal important differences in the pattern of consumer expenditure by different income classes as well as in the inter-regional market prices that consumers in different regions will face. In determining the accounting wage rate in particular (see the final section in this appendix) it will be necessary to have more specific consumption conversion factors for different income groups in different regions. However, given the breakdown of the expenditure at market prices of these groups, once again the market value of the component items can be revalued in terms of accounting prices, and the specific consumption conversion factors for the particular groups and/or regions can be determined. This is done in tables 32 and 33, the notes to which explain the various accounting ratios used in the revaluation of market values. The consumption conversion factors derived were summarised in table 1B.

DISTRIBUTIONAL WEIGHTING

The net benefits from an investment project normally accrue to particular groups at various points in time. We therefore have to make commensurable the gains and losses incurred both intratemporally (as amongst contemporaries) and intertemporally (as between different generations). For this we clearly need weights. The simplest weights are obviously unity for every gain or loss—that is, we do not take any account of the intertemporal and intratemporal distributional effects of investment projects.[1] This would be valid if the social value of the gains were the same irrespective of whom they accrued to, or if government could neutralise the distributional effects of investment projects by neutral tax–subsidy policies. As the latter are not likely to be feasible, and given that the social marginal utility of incremental gains in income are likely to differ for people at different income levels, it becomes necessary to take account of the distributional effects of investment projects. The choice of projects (given the fiscal constraint) now becomes an instrument for influencing the distribution of income (both inter- and intratemporally) through the differential income distribution effects of different projects.

There can be at least three dimensions to this problem of distributional weights.

Intertemporal distribution

First, there is the problem of intertemporal income distribution. Investment is a means of changing the time-stream of consumption, as it normally entails sacrificing current consumption (increasing current savings) to provide more consumption in the future. Since with the normal processes of growth we expect future generations to be richer than current ones, an increase in investment will entail transferring income (consumption) from the currently "poor" to future "rich" generations, and as normally we assume that the marginal utility of consumption (income) declines with rises in consumption (income), clearly 1 peso transferred to a future generation will be less valuable in terms of "utility" than if the same 1 peso were consumed by the current generation. This implies that future consumption will be less valuable socially than current consumption, and hence will have to be discounted to put it on a par with current consumption. The discount rate will

---

[1] For a strong plea for not taking distributional effects into account, see A. C. Harberger: "Three basic postulates of applied welfare economics: An interpretive essay", in *The Journal of Economic Literature* (Menasha, Wis.), Sep. 1971.

obviously depend upon how rich future generations are expected to be, independently of the effects flowing from our particular investment project, as well as on how the social marginal utility of consumption (income) alters with changes in income and consumption.

We therefore need to have some estimate of the future rate of growth of consumption, as well as of the specifications of a social utility (welfare) function. The simplest and most widely used social welfare function for valuing intertemporal changes in consumption is a constant elasticity utility function, which has dated consumption per head as its arguments. The rate at which consumption accruing between two periods t and $(t + 1)$ should be discounted is labelled the *consumption rate of interest* (CRI_t), between these two dates.[1] The CRI will then be given by

$$CRI_t = (U_t'/U_{t+1}') - 1 \qquad (4)$$

where the U' represents the marginal utility of aggregate consumption per head at the two dates. Given an intertemporal social welfare function of the form

$$U_t' = K/C_t^e \qquad (5)$$

where e is the assumed constant elasticity of social marginal utility and C_t is consumption per head at date t and that, by definition, the growth rate of consumption per head (G_t)

$$G_t = (C_{t+1} - C_t)/C_t, \qquad (6)$$

then from (4) to (6) it follows that

$$CRI_t = (1 + G_t)^e - 1. \qquad (7)$$

From the national accounts data we find that the annual growth rate of real aggregate consumption between 1960 and 1972 was about 4 per cent. Given the rate of growth of population of about 3 per cent, we get the real growth rate of consumption per head during this period as about 1 per cent.

If we assume that in the near future the same growth of consumption per head will be realised, then assuming that the elasticity of marginal utility lies between 1 and 2,[2] we have the value of the CRI from (7) for the Philippines as

$$CRI_a = 2 \text{ per cent (assuming } e = 2);$$

$$CRI_b = 1 \text{ per cent (assuming } e = 1).$$

These estimates show the rate at which future consumption should be discounted relative to present consumption. If the current productivity of investment were such that the rate of transformation of present into future consumption (the social return to investment (SR)) were also no better than $(1 + CRI)$, there would be no social justification for increasing current savings and investment. If, however, SR > CRI, then assuming that 1 peso is invested today it would yield a perpetuity whose present value would be SR/CRI, in terms of present consumption. Thus it is clear that an increase in current savings and investment would be socially desirable.

It is commonly believed that most developing countries suffer from a shortage of savings, in the sense that governments feel that they cannot raise enough savings to bring the value of the SR and the CRI together. In such a situation, clearly the savings–consumption distribution of the net benefits of investment projects could be of impor-

---

[1] See Little and Mirrlees: *Social cost benefit analysis*, op. cit. The CRI is also known as the social rate of discount (see UNIDO: *Guidelines for project evaluation*, op. cit.).
[2] See Deepak Lal: *Wells and welfare* (Paris, OECD Development Centre, 1972) for arguments why this range is plausible. It should be noted that the value of e is essentially a social value judgement. Relatively higher values of e imply a greater concern with equality.

tance in breaking this "savings bottle-neck". Savings will then be more important, in governmental eyes, than an equivalent amount of present consumption. This premium, designated as s,[1] will depend upon the divergence between the SR and the CRI, and the time (T) it will take the divergence to disappear.

Remembering that the SR is defined in terms of present consumption, and that our numeraire is future consumption (savings), we can revalue the SR in terms of savings to obtain what Little and Mirrlees call the *accounting rate of interes* (ARI).[2] They also derive a formula for determining the current value of s (the current premium on savings) in terms of the existing divergence between the current ARI and CRI, and on the assumption that this divergence diminishes linearly until it disappears T years hence. Then

$$s_1 = [1 + 1/2(\text{ARI}_1 - \text{CRI}_1)]^T. \tag{8}$$

To determine s_1, the intertemporal weight to be attached to present consumption in terms of savings (future consumption)—our numeraire, we therefore need estimates of the ARI, the CRI and T.

Estimates for the CRI have already been given above. It has been estimated that the average rate of return at world prices (and hence in terms of our numeraire) is 15 per cent for large-scale manufacturing in the Philippines.[3] We assume, therefore, that the marginal rate of return for the whole economy (at "world" prices) is about 12, and this will be the ARI.

There is very little to go on to estimate T. We arbitrarily assume that $T = 30$ years. On the alternative assumptions about e, the value of s, and hence the CRI is

$e = 2$

$s = 4$	CRI = 2 per cent	ARI = 12 per cent

$e = 1$

$s = 5$	CRI = 1 per cent	ARI = 12 per cent

This implies that if $e = 2$, $s = 4$ units of present consumption are worth 1 unit of savings (consumption forgone). Hence the value of marginal aggregate current consumption increases in terms of our numeraire (savings) is simply $1/s = 1/4$ times their nominal value.[4]

It should also be noted that the correct discount rate, given our numeraire for making intertemporal accounting values commensurable, will be the ARI. Hence the discount rate to be used, for social cost-benefit analysis on the lines of this study, will be 12 per cent.

---

[1] See Little and Mirrlees, *Social cost benefit analysis*, op. cit.

[2] ibid. For a two-period case, assuming that SR $= r$, and that θ per cent of the benefits are saved and $(1 - \theta)$ per cent consumed in any year, and s_1 is the premium attached to savings in year 1, we have $\text{ARI}_1 = r[\theta + (1 - \theta)/s_1]$.

[3] See ILO: *Sharing in development ...*, op. cit., special paper 10: "Private and social rates of return in manufacturing".

[4] Given our estimated values of the CRI and the ARI, the value of s is unfortunately quite sensitive to higher values of the estimate of T, as the following table shows:

T	e	s
20	1	3
20	2	3
30	1	5
30	2	4
50	1	15
50	2	12

Distribution within generations

The second type of distributional effect occurs within the members of the same generation. How can we make commensurable the income gains and losses of contemporaries? Assuming again that we can employ a constant elasticity social utility function, we can derive these weights as follows.[1]

Let the social valuation function for valuing changes in income of income group Y_i be

$$U'(Y_i) = k \cdot Y_i^{-e} \tag{9}$$

where U' is social marginal utility and k is a constant of scale which converts the private "utils" accruing to particular income groups into social utils.

We now make use of a property of certain "positive" measures of the size distribution of income (the Gini coefficient): namely that, with a given distribution of income, an equiproportionate rise in all incomes raises the mean income but leaves the value of the distributional measure unchanged. We define our social utils in terms of this "distribution–neutrality" property, by making the change in total private income socially valuable at par, if it is distribution neutral: that is, if there is an equiproportionate rise in all incomes of θ per cent, this will result in a rise in social utils (V) of

$$V = \theta n \bar{C} \tag{10}$$

where n is the number of incomes and $\bar{C}$ is the arithmetical mean income of the population.

However, in like manner, it should be possible to derive this change in social utils (V) from our general social valuation function (9)—that is, V is also given by

$$V = \int_0^\infty f(C) \int_C^{(1+\theta)C} kY^{-e}dY \cdot dC = [k \cdot n/(e-1)][(1+\theta)^{e-1} - 1]/[1+\theta)^{e-1}C_{e-1}^*] \tag{11}$$

where $f(C)$ is the frequency of those obtaining income (consumption) C, and

$$1/C_{e-1}^* = (1/n) \int_0^\infty f(C)C^{-(e-1)}dC,$$

that is C_{e-1}^* is the harmonic mean of degree $(e-1)$ of the income (consumption) distribution, and n is the number of incomes.[2]

From equations (10) and (11) it follows that

$$k = \bar{C}C_{e-1}^*[(e-1)\theta(1+\theta)^{e-1}]/[(1+\theta)^{e-1} - 1]. \tag{12}$$

For a marginal change in income (consumption) in the limit $\theta \to 0$, and[3]

$$k = \bar{C}C_{e-1}^* \tag{13}$$

---

[1] The derivation is due to F. Seton: *Shadow wages in the Chilean economy* (Paris, OECD Development Centre, 1972). The justification given for the derivation differs from Seton's and is based on Deepak Lal: *Distributional weights in project analysis*, Staff working paper 130, revised version (Washington, DC, World Bank, 1972).

[2] The result presented is valid for $e > 1$. If $e = 1$, equation (11) becomes $V = k \log(1+\theta)n$.

[3] For $e = 1$, we get $k = \dfrac{\theta}{-\log(1+\theta)}C$, which as $\theta \to 0$ yields $k = \bar{C}$, and the valuation function becomes $U'(Y_i) = \bar{C}/Y_i$.

Table 34.   Distributional weights (all-Philippines)

Annual income per head (pesos)	$e = 1$ $s = 5$		$e = 2$ $s = 4$	
	w_i	d_i	w_i	d_i
408·2	1·5255	0·3051	0·9987	0·2477
481·0	1·2945	0·2589	0·7119	0·1779
600·0	1·0377	0·2075	0·4575	0·1143
734·5	0·8477	0·1695	0·3053	0·0763
800·0	0·7783	0·1556	0·2573	0·0643
900·0	0·6918	0·1383	0·2033	0·0508
1 000·0	0·6226	0·1245	0·1647	0·0411
1 100·0	0·5660	0·1132	0·1361	0·0340
1 200·0	0·5188	0·1037	0·1143	0·0285
1 300·0	0·4789	0·0957	0·0974	0·0243
1 400·0	0·4447	0·0889	0·0840	0·0210
1 500·0	0·4151	0·0830	0·0732	0·0183
1 600·0	0·3728	0·0745	0·0590	0·0147

Key:
e = elasticity of marginal utility;
s = premium on savings;
w_i = intertemporal distributional weight; and
d_i = intra-cum-intertemporal distributional weight.

and hence, substituting equation (13) in equation (9), we have as our social valuation function

$$U'(Y_i) = C C^*_{e-1}/Y^e_i. \tag{13a}$$

For a marginal change in the income of income group Y_i, therefore, the social value of its income change will be just $w_i = \bar{C} C^*_{e-1}/Y^e_i$ times the nominal change in income.

The complete distributional weight d_i, which takes account of both intertemporal and intratemporal distribution, will be

$$d_i = w_{i/S} = \bar{C} C^*_{e-1}/Y^e_i \cdot s.$$

The values of w_i and d_i, calculated for various income levels for the Philippines, are given in table 34 for $e = 2$ and $e = 1$. Tables 36 and 37 give the values of C and C^*_{e-1}. The latter was calculated from the income distribution data given in the family income and expenditures survey.

Inter-regional distribution

Third, the social evaluation of the inter-regional distribution of income gains and losses is also likely to be important for the Philippines. Once again, it is assumed that government cannot use neutral tax–subsidy measures to neutralise the inter-regional distributional impact of projects. We can take account of this distributional aspect by an extension of the argument in the preceding subsection.

We now follow a two-step procedure. We first convert changes in the private utils accruing to income recipients in region z into that region's distribution–neutral units. The second step is to convert the changes in the region's distribution–neutral units into

Table 35.   Distributional weights (regional[1]) ($e = 2$; $s = 4$)

Annual income per head (pesos) Y_i	Region I		Region II		Region III		Region IV		Region V	
	w_{ji}	d_{ji}	w_{ji}	d_{ji}	w_{ji}	d_{ji}	w_{ji}	d_{ji}	w_{ji}	d_{ji}
408·17	0·4232	0·1058	0·9987	0·2496	1·3787	0·3446	0·7983	0·1995	0·7605	0·1901
481·0	0·3047	0·0761	0·7191	0·1797	0·9927	0·2481	0·5749	0·1437	0·5476	0·1369
600·0	0·1958	0·0489	0·4622	0·1155	0·6380	0·1595	0·3694	0·0923	0·3519	0·0879
734·5	0·1307	0·0326	0·3084	0·0771	0·4257	0·1064	0·2465	0·0616	0·2348	0·0587
800·0	0·1101	0·0275	0·2599	0·0649	0·3588	0·0897	0·2078	0·0519	0·1979	0·0494
900·0	0·0870	0·0217	0·2054	0·0513	0·2835	0·0708	0·1642	0·0410	0·1564	0·0391
1 000·0	0·0705	0·0176	0·1663	0·0415	0·2296	0·0574	0·1330	0·0332	0·1267	0·0316
1 100·0	0·0582	0·0145	0·1375	0·0343	0·1898	0·0474	0·1099	0·0274	0·1047	0·0261
1 200·0	0·0489	0·0122	0·1155	0·0288	0·1595	0·0398	0·0923	0·0230	0·0879	0·0219
1 300·0	0·0417	0·0104	0·0984	0·0246	0·1359	0·0339	0·0787	0·0196	0·0749	0·0187
1 400·0	0·0359	0·0089	0·0848	0·0212	0·1171	0·0292	0·0678	0·0169	0·0646	0·0161
1 500·0	0·0313	0·0078	0·0739	0·0184	0·1020	0·0255	0·0591	0·0147	0·0563	0·0140
1 670·0	0·0252	0·0063	0·0596	0·0149	0·0823	0·0205	0·0476	0·0119	0·0454	0·0113

Annual income per head (pesos) Y_i	Region VI		Region VII		Region VIII		Region IX		Region X	
	w_{ji}	d_{ji}	w_{ji}	d_{ji}	w_{ji}	d_{ji}	w_{ji}	d_{ji}	w_{ji}	d_{ji}
408·17	1·1834	0·2958	1·0277	0·2569	1·2931	0·3232	1·0760	0·2690	0·9211	0·2302
481·0	0·8522	0·2130	0·7400	0·1850	0·9311	0·2327	0·7748	0·1937	0·6632	0·1658
600·0	0·5477	0·1369	0·4756	0·1189	0·5984	0·1496	0·4979	0·1244	0·4262	0·1065
734·5	0·3654	0·0913	0·3173	0·0793	0·3993	0·0998	0·3323	0·0830	0·2844	0·0711
800·0	0·3080	0·0770	0·2675	0·0668	0·3366	0·0841	0·2801	0·0700	0·2397	0·0599
900·0	0·2434	0·0608	0·2113	0·0528	0·2659	0·0664	0·2213	0·0553	0·1894	0·0473
1 000·0	0·1971	0·0480	0·1712	0·0428	0·2154	0·0538	0·1792	0·0448	0·1534	0·0383
1 100·0	0·1629	0·0407	0·1415	0·0353	0·1780	0·0445	0·1481	0·0370	0·1268	0·0317
1 200·0	0·1369	0·0342	0·1189	0·0297	0·1496	0·0374	0·1244	0·0311	0·1065	0·0266
1 300·0	0·1166	0·0291	0·1013	0·0253	0·1274	0·0318	0·1060	0·0265	0·0908	0·0227
1 400·0	0·1005	0·0251	0·0873	0·0218	0·1099	0·0274	0·0915	0·0229	0·0782	0·0195
1 500·0	0·0876	0·0219	0·0760	0·0190	0·0957	0·0289	0·0796	0·0199	0·0682	0·0170
1 670·0	0·0706	0·0176	0·0613	0·0153	0·0772	0·0193	0·0642	0·0160	0·0550	0·0137

[1] For names of regions, see table 1B.

Key:

e = elasticity of marginal utility;

s = premium on savings;

w_{ji} = weight when only intratemporal distribution is taken into account; and

d_{ji} = weight when both intra- and intertemporal distribution are taken into account.

national distribution–neutral units. The marginal change in social welfare, taking account of both inter-regional and intra-regional distribution as a result of a marginal increase in the income of group Y_{iz} in region z, will then be given by

$$W_{iz} = U'(Y_{iz}) = \frac{\bar{C}_r C^*_{r(e-1)}}{\bar{C}_z^e} \cdot \frac{\bar{C}_z C^*_{z(e-1)}}{Y_{iz}^e}$$

Table 36. Number of families and average annual household income by income class, Philippines, 1971

Income class (pesos per year)	No. of families (thousands)	Average annual household income (pesos)
Under 500	329	337
500–999	767	754
1 000–1 499	773	1 250
1 500–1 999	748	1 743
2 000–2 499	611	2 245
2 500–2 999	517	2 744
3 000–3 999	794	3 446
4 000–4 999	475	4 452
5 000–5 999	316	5 455
6 000–7 999	403	6 866
8 000–9 999	226	8 909
10 000–14 999	234	11 994
15 000–19 999	71	17 092
20 000 +	81	31 746

Computed values (assuming household size is six members):
$\bar{C} = 622 \cdot 67$; $\quad C^*_{e-1} = 264 \cdot 55$ (for $e = 2$)
where
$\bar{C}$ = arithmetical mean;
C^*_{e-1} = harmonic mean of the income distribution of degree $(e - 1)$; and
e = elasticity of marginal utility.

Source: Bureau of the Census and Statistics: *Family income and expenditures survey, 1971*, table 2.

where
$\bar{C}_r$ = arithmetical mean of the inter-regional incomes (national income per head);
$C^*_{r(e-1)}$ = harmonic mean of degree $(e - 1)$ of the inter-regional incomes;
$\bar{C}_z$ = mean regional income in region z; and
$C^*_{z(e-1)}$ = harmonic mean of degree $(e - 1)$ of the distribution of income in region z.

Table 37 gives the data used on inter-regional incomes. As data were not readily available for the distribution of income within regions, $C^*_{z(e-1)}$ was assumed to be equal to the harmonic mean of the national income distribution (for all z).

Table 35 gives the resulting estimates of w_i and d_i for different income groups in the various regions.

ACCOUNTING WAGES

Analytical framework

For analytical purposes we divide the economy into three major sectors: an agricultural sector, an unorganised urban sector and an organised urban sector. The market wage rates for unskilled labourers in the rural and unorganised urban sectors are assumed to be competitively determined, whilst the rate in the organised sector could be institutionally fixed above the competitive supply price of unskilled labour to that sector. Furthermore, we assume that relative wage differentials within each of these sectors reflect skill differentials and relative value marginal productivities at market prices of the various skills, and hence the respective private returns to human capital formation for

Table 37.   Total number of families and average annual household income by region, 1971

Region[1]	No. of families (thousands)	Average annual household income (pesos)
I	525	7 785
II	346	3 299
III	260	2 390
IV	855	4 127
V	869	4 332
VI	496	2 784
VII	670	3 206
VIII	980	2 548
IX	522	3 062
X	825	3 577

[1] For names of regions, see table 1B.

Computed values (assuming household size is six members):
$\bar{C}_r = 622 \cdot 67$; $C^*_{\bar{H}(e-1)} = 555 \cdot 5$ (for $e = 2$);
$\bar{C}^*_z = 264 \cdot 5$; and
$\bar{C}_z$:

I $= 1297 \cdot 5$;	II $= 549 \cdot 83$;	III $= 398 \cdot 33$;
IV $= 687 \cdot 83$;	V $= 722 \cdot 00$;	VI $= 464 \cdot 00$;
VII $= 534 \cdot 33$;	VIII $= 424 \cdot 67$;	IX $= 510 \cdot 33$;
X $= 596 \cdot 17$		

where
$\bar{C}_r$ = arithmetical mean of mean inter-regional incomes per head;
$C^*_{\bar{H}(e-1)}$ = harmonic mean of degree $(e-1)$ of mean inter-regional income per head;
$\bar{C}^*_z$ = harmonic mean of intra-regional incomes per head which is assumed to be the same for all regions, and equal to $C^*_{(e-1)}$; and
$\bar{C}_z$ = mean income per head in region z.

Source: Bureau of the Census and Statistics: *Family income and expenditures survey, 1971*, table 1.

each particular level of skill. Furthermore, if we assume that the social costs of training (skill formation) are borne by the private individuals themselves (that is, private and social costs of training are identical), the private returns to human capital formation would also represent the social returns if the private and social rates of discount were the same. Then the intrasectoral wage differentials would also represent the relative social benefits from the differing skill levels. Although we lack the data to test their validity for the Philippines,[1] we shall nevertheless make these assumptions. This considerably simplifies our task of determining the shadow wage rate (SWR) for any particular type of labour, since the SWR of each type of labour within our three-sector classification will be directly linked to the SWR of unskilled labour in that sector. Thus, for instance, if we want to determine the SWR of labour type j in sector i, and we know that the market wage for type j labour (W_{ij}) is proportionately higher than the market wage for unskilled labour (W_{iu}) in sector i by $k = W_{ij}/W_{iu}$, then

$$\mathrm{SWR}_{ij} = \frac{W_{iu}}{A_i}(k-1) + \mathrm{SWR}_{iu}$$

where A_i is the accounting ratio for converting the market value of the sector i's output into accounting prices. Our major task, therefore is to determine the SWR for unskilled labour in the rural sector (SWR_{ru}), the unorganised urban sector (SWR_{su}) and the organised urban sector (SWR_{mu}), where the first subscript refers to the sector $(r = \text{rural},$

---

[1] This is clearly a fruitful area for further research.

s = service/unorganised, m = manufacturing/organised) and the second subscript stands for the type of labour (u = unskilled).

To determine the three unskilled SWRs, we consider hypothetical projects in each of our three sectors which increase the demand for unskilled labour by one additional man in that sector, and ask: (*a*) from where the extra labour to meet this additional demand will come; and (*b*) what are the consequences on social welfare in terms of our numeraire savings valued in foreign exchange.

The simplest case

It has traditionally been assumed that, in labour-surplus economies, additional demand for labour anywhere in the economy will ultimately be met by drawing upon the "surplus" labour in agriculture, and hence the flow of labour is assumed to be from the rural to the other sectors. Thus an increase in demand for one man in the organised sector will ultimately lead to the withdrawal of one agricultural worker. We shall start with this assumption but shall modify it later to take account of certain other complications.

The SWR, then, will have to take account of three main components. Initially, we assume that market prices for goods coincide with their accounting prices. Then, first, there will be the output forgone (Y) in agriculture by withdrawing the agricultural labourer. Second, the agricultural worker may need to be compensated for various psychic disutilities and real resource costs of moving (which should be included as a resource cost with the output forgone), which make his supply price (L) to the new employer higher than the output forgone (Y). Third, the actual wage (W) paid to the worker in his new employment may be higher than even his supply price, and is often likely to be higher than the income (wage) he received before. The difference between his current wage (W) and output forgone (Y), provides him (and possibly his relatives in the agricultural sector if he came from a family farm with equal work and income sharing) with a rise in income, part of which will be saved and the rest consumed. If a percentage c of the increased income is consumed ($1 - c$ is then saved); this will commit the economy to an increase in aggregate consumption, and hence will adversely affect its aggregate consumption/savings balance. If the current premium on savings vis-à-vis consumption is s (see the preceding section), the social benefit from the increase in consumption is $c(W - Y)/s$.

This, however, assumes that we make no distinction between increases in current consumption of "poor" and "rich" workers. Clearly, as argued in the preceding section, we must also weight the increase in consumption of one unskilled worker by the relevant distributional weight w/s. The composite weight, taking account of both urban and intertemporal distribution, is then simply the relevant $d_L = w_L/s$. The social benefit from the worker's increase in consumption is then simply $d_L c(W - Y)$. Thus, from the social cost of increasing the worker's consumption $c(W - Y)$ we must subtract the social benefit (in terms of our numeraire) of this increase to obtain the *net* social cost of the increase in consumption, which is simply

$$c(W - Y)(1 - d_L).$$

We can now put the three components of the SWR together. These are:
(1) Output forgone = Y.
(2) Change in disutility of effort = $(L - Y)$ in terms of consumption.[1]
(3) Net social cost of increased consumption = $c(W - Y)(1 - d_L)$.

---

[1] See Lal: "Disutility of effort...", op. cit., for the derivation. The argument is that utility maximising workers at the margin will equate the disutility of increased effort with the utility from the increased incomes this extra work makes possible.

The consumption equivalent of (2) must first be converted into its savings equivalent which, again taking account of both intratemporal and intertemporal weighting, will be $d_L(L - Y)$. It can be argued[1] that this change in the disutility of effort does not represent a social cost, and to allow for this possibility we introduce a social valuation parameter λ, which converts the savings equivalent of private disutilities of effort into their social equivalent value, with $\lambda = 0$ (when private disutilities of effort are not valued at all) and $\lambda = 1$ (when they are valued socially at par).

Finally, we must take account of the divergences between market and accounting prices for various goods. This implies that the values at market prices given in the three components of the SWR above have to be converted into their accounting price equivalents by using the appropriate accounting ratios (see the first two sections of this appendix). Thus, first, the output forgone (Y) has to be converted into its accounting value by using the relevant accounting ratio for that output; if it is, say, rice, the output forgone is Y/A_R. Second, the changes in consumption at market prices under (2) and (3) have to be converted into their accounting price equivalents by using the consumption conversion ratio for the particular type of labour (income group). If labour of type j is being considered, the relevant consumption conversion factor will be C_j (see "Consumption conversion factors" above).

Thus the final value of the SWR, asssuming that Y refers to rice, is

$$\text{SWR} = Y/A_R + c(W - Y)(1 - d_L)/C_j + \lambda(L - Y)d_L/C_j$$

or

$$\text{SWR} = Y/A_R + [c(W - Y)(1 - d_L) + \lambda(L - Y)d_L]/C_j \qquad (14)$$

Some complications

Bidding up wages

We now introduce some complications. We first remove the simplifying assumption that the ultimate effect of an increase in demand for a particular type of labour would be a withdrawal of an equivalent number of rural workers. We now assume that part of the increase in demand for labour of type j is met from within the industry using that type of labour by bidding up its wage by ΔW_j;[2] that is, we now assume that, if there is a unit increase in demand in industry j, a proportion ΔL_j of this demand is met from within the industry by bidding up wages and the remainder $(1 - \Delta L_j)$ is met ultimately drawing upon rural labour. The SWR for the latter is given by equation (14). What about the former?

The "extra" ΔL_j workers have been "released" by industry j by bidding up its wage to ΔW_j. This has two major consequences. The first is that the industry "loses" the marginal product of these ΔL_j workers, whose market value $\Delta L_j . W_j$ (where W_j is the wage in industry j before it increased its employment). The social cost of this output forgone is simply $\Delta L_j W_j/A_j$, where A_j is the accounting ratio for the output of industry j.

The second consequence is that, as a result of the bidding up of the wages by ΔW_j, there will be a transfer of income from employers and/or consumers to the workers in industry j which will approximately be equal to $\Delta W_j . L_j$ (where L_j is the total initial employment in industry j). If for simplicity's sake we assume that this transfer is

---

[1] Lal: "Disutility of effort . . .", op. cit.

[2] This complication was introduced by Scott and is analysed by him in M. FG. Scott, J. D. MacArthur and D. M. G. Newbery: *Project appraisal in practice: The Little–Mirrlees method applied in Kenya* (London, Heinemann, 1976), and the following paragraphs are based on his analysis.

from "rich" employers to "poor" j industry workers,[1] we have to weight this income change by the relevant distributional weights. Before doing so, however, we must take account of the differential savings of the two groups. If the average propensity to consume of the employers is c_{ej} and that of the workers is c_{wj}, and $c_{ej} < c_{wj}$ as seems plausible, the net change in consumption will be $\Delta W_j L_j (c_{wj} - c_{ej})$. Thus, if the distributional weight for j industry employers is d_{ej} and that for its workers is d_{wj}, the income transfer represents a social cost of $\Delta W_j L_j (d_{ej} c_{ej} - d_{wj} c_{wj})$, which will be negative, given that $d_{wj} > d_{ej}$, and this term is therefore (as we would expect) a social benefit.

We thus have the social cost of releasing ΔL_j workers from the industry j by bidding up its wages as

$$\text{SWR}\Delta L_j = \Delta L_j W_j / A_j + \Delta W_j L_j (d_{ej} c_{ej} - d_{wj} c_{wj}).$$

Defining the price (wage) elasticity of demand for workers in the j industry E_j as

$$E_j = \frac{\Delta L_j}{\Delta W_j} \cdot \frac{W_j}{L_j}$$

we have

$$\text{SWR}\Delta L_j = \Delta L_j W_j \left[\frac{1}{A_j} - \frac{1}{E_j} (d_{wj} c_{wj} - d_{ej} c_{ej}) \right] \tag{15}$$

and the SWR for increasing employment in industry j will then just be the sum of the SWR for $(1 - \Delta L_j)$ rural workers from equations (14) plus (15), that is

$$\text{SWR}_j = (1 - \Delta L_j)[c_j(W_j - Y)(1 - d_{wj}) + \lambda(L - Y)d_{wj}]/c_j$$

$$+ \Delta L_j W_j \left[\frac{1}{A_j} - \frac{1}{E_j} (d_{wj} c_{wj} - d_{ej} c_{ej}) \right]. \tag{16}$$

Rural–urban migration

The final complication we introduce is the possibility that, as a result of creating an additional job in the urban sector, more than one rural worker migrates to that sector.[2] We initially assume that there is no bidding up of wages in the sectors in which extra employment is being created. Then, assuming (a) for simplicity's sake, that a one-period migration model is a fair approximation to reality;[3] (b) that the migrant's supply price L is made up of his income forgone a and the costs of moving m, which include any psychic disutilities of moving (so $L = a + m$); (c) that the migrant moves with the expectation of getting a relatively high wage job in the organised sector at the wage W_{mu} but whilst searching for such a job he can nevertheless find some employment in the unorganised urban sector at the wage W_{su}; (d) that the probability P of getting an organised sector job is given by the number of vacancies V_t in each period divided by the number of job-seekers, the "unemployed" U_t, then the number of migrants M who are drawn in as a result of one additional organised sector job will be $M = 1/P_e$, where P_e is the equilibrium probability of getting an urban sector job and is determined as follows: each migrant equates the total costs of migration, given by L, with the expected benefits $(PW_{mu} + (1 - P)W_{su})$ where P is the probability of getting an organised sector job.[4] Hence in equilibrium

---

[1] For cases where this assumption is relaxed and the effect on consumers too is taken into account, see Scott et al., op. cit.

[2] This part is based on Lal: "Disutility of effort ...", op. cit.

[3] Strictly speaking, the migration decision should be considered to be a multi-period decision in which the present value of the costs of migration should at the margin be equal to the present value of the benefits from migration. If, however, as is likely, migrants have high subjective rates of time discount (fairly short time horizons), the use of a single-period migration decision model may not be invalid.

[4] For these and the succeeding derivations, see Lal: "Disutility of effort ...", op. cit.

$$L = PW_{mu} + (1 - P)W_{su}$$

and from this the equilibrium value of P (Pe) is

$$Pe = (L - W_{su})/(W_{mu} - W_{su}).$$

The number of migrants M who will move with the creation of an additional organised sector job is therefore

$$M = 1/Pe = (W_{mu} - W_{su})/(L - W_{su}).$$

The SWR for each of these rural migrants is given by equation (14) and hence the SWR for an additional job in the organised sector will just be Mx (14) and

$$SWR_{mu} = Mx (14).$$

The effects on the SWR in the organised or unorganised sector, with bidding up of wages in that sector, can also be easily deduced. If the unorganised/organised sector wage is bid up by ΔW_{su}, this will affect Pe and hence M. The SWR will therefore be

$$SWR_{su} = ([W_{mu} - (W_{su} + \Delta W_{su})]/[L - (W_{su} + \Delta W_{su})]) \times (14)$$

or

$$SWR_{mu} = ([W_{mu} + \Delta W_{mu}) - W_{su}]/(L - W_{su})) \times (14). \tag{17}$$

We shall now make estimates of these various components of the SWR for rural, urban unorganised and urban organised unskilled labour in the Philippines.

Farm labour

We need an estimate of the output forgone (valued at border prices) by employing a rural worker. This rural worker could previously have been a family worker or a wage employee. If he was a family worker on a farm without any hired labour, and equal work and income sharing was practised on the family farm, then the output forgone by removing him from the farm would not be given by his marginal product.[1] If, however, he

Table 38. Area and size of farms by major crop category, 1960

Crop	No. of farms (thousands)	Area (thousands) of hectares	Average-sized farms (hectares)	Percentage of total area in farms of 10 hectares and over
Sugar-cane	17·8	249·4	13·9	80
Abaca	36·0	209·0	5·8	49
Coconut	440·3	1 938·6	4·4	38
Palay	1 041·9	3 112·1	3·0	20
Maize	378·8	949·3	2·5	20
Tobacco	22·9	38·4	1·7	8
Others	228·5	1 275·7	5·6	.
All farms	2 166·2	7 777·5	3·6	33

Source: Bureau of the Census and Statistics: *Census of the Philippines, 1960; Agriculture*, Vol. II: *Summary report* (Manila, 1963).

---

[1] See A. K. Sen: "Peasants and dualism with or without surplus labor", in *The Journal of Political Economy* (Chicago), Oct. 1966; and idem: *Employment, technology and development*, op. cit.

Table 39.   Number and area of farms by type of land tenure, 1960

Tenure status	No. of farms	Percentage of total no. of farms	Area (hectares)	Percentage of total land area
Full owner	967 725	44·67	4 133 276	53·18
Part owner	310 944	14·35	1 139 956	14·67
Tenant	864 538	39·91	2 000 201	25·73
Manager	2 487	0·11	365 309	4·70
Other forms of tenure	20 522	0·95	133 742	1·72
Total	2 166 216	100·00	7 772 484	100·0

Source: Bureau of the Census and Statistics: *Census of the Philippines, 1960: Agriculture*, Vol. II: *Summary report*, pp. 8–9.

Table 40.   Number and area of tenanted farms by type of tenancy, 1960

Type of tenant	No. of tenanted farms	Percentage of total no. of tenanted farms	Area (hectares)	Percentage of total land area of tenanted farms
Cash	13 506	1·56	47 008	2·35
Fixed amount of produce	34 145	3·95	88 911	4·45
Share of produce	745 426	86·22	1 677 857	83·88
Cash and fixed amount of produce	693	0·08	3 676	0·18
Cash and share of produce	10 847	1·25	34 083	1·70
Rent-free	29 816	3·45	55 918	2·80
Others	30 105	3·48	92 748	4·64
	864 538	100·00	2 000 201	100·0

Source: Bureau of the Census and Statistics: *Census of the Philippines, 1960: Agriculture*, Vol. II: *Summary report*, pp. 8–9.

Table 41.   Distribution of landowners and of area of tenanted landholdings sown to rice and maize, by size of holding, in nine pilot municipalities,[1] 1973

Size of holding (hectares)	Percentage of total number of landowners	Percentage of total area
24·0 and above	2·3	35·6
12·0–23·9	3·4	13·0
7·0–11·9	5·8	12·3
Below 7·0	*88·5*	*39·1*
5·0– 6·9	6·0	8·1
3·0– 4·9	15·2	11·0
Below 3·0	*67·3*	*20·0*
All sizes	100·0	100·0

[1] Calamba and Biñan, in Laguna; Bongabon, Zaragoza and Guimba, in Nueva Ecija; Pototan and Dingle, in Iloilo; Plaridel, in Bulacan; and San Mateo, in Isabela.

Source: Department of Agrarian Reform, cited in ILO: *Sharing in development* . . . , op. cit., p. 480.

was a family farm worker on a farm which also used hired labour, the marginal product of hired labour (which would equal the agricultural wage rate) would also be the marginal product of family labour, and the agricultural wage rate would measure the output forgone at market prices of both family and hired labour.

We therefore need some information on landless labour and the proportion of farms which make no use of hired labour in the Philippines.

Data on landless labour in the Philippines were not readily available.[1] Tables 38 to 41 give the relevant information on the area under different crops and tenurial status. From these it appears that: (a) one-half of the cropped area is accounted for by palay and maize; (b) nearly half the cropped area is under some form of tenancy arrangement; and (c) most of the landowners owning palay and maize land have holdings below 7 hectares.

Furthermore, there is a considerable body of survey evidence for the Philippines[2] which shows that there is no difference in the productivity of farms (yields per hectare) between different tenure groups. It appears[3] that it is common for landowners to take many of the crucial factor input decisions (e.g. quantity of fertiliser use, etc.), as well as sharing part of the costs in some forms of tenancy, jointly with their tenants. Furthermore, given the small size of the average palay landowner's holding, it is relatively easy for him to supervise his tenants' work (unlike absentee landlords). Given this supervision, and the complementarity between certain produced inputs (e.g. fertilisers) and own-family labour, the total labour input (and other factor inputs) may not be different on different types of farms in the Philippines. This would explain the lack of any differences in productivity across tenure groups, and hence bear out Cheung's thesis[4] of the "efficiency" of share-cropping under certain conditions.

Given the same productivity per hectare on different types of palay and maize farms, and hence implicitly the same marginal product of labour on all farms, we need not, for the Philippines, distinguish between the amounts of output forgone if farm labour is drawn from different types of farm. Output forgone would be the same irrespective of the type of farm from which the labour was drawn.

The next question, therefore, is whether the agricultural wage rate gives an adequate measure of the value of the marginal product of labour, and hence the output forgone by withdrawing an agricultural labourer.

For this purpose a digression on the special institutional features of the Philippines labour market for palay is necessary. Takahashi has studied the particular labour market of a village in Central Luzon.[5] He found that share-croppers were more like agricultural

---

[1] However, a 1952 survey showed that of the total labour force of sample *barrios*, 47 per cent were labourers (but this probably included family labour, given the peculiar local practice of exchanging such labour) while only 22 per cent were farmers and tenants. See G. Rivera and R. McMillan: *The rural Philippines* (Manila, 1953).

[2] See ILO: *Sharing in development . . .*, op. cit., special paper 5: "Agrarian reform".

[3] J. P. Estanislao: "A note on differential farm productivity by tenure", in *Philippine Economic Journal*, 1965, No. 1; V. W. Ruttan: "Tenure and productivity of Philippine rice-producing farms", in *Philippine Economic Journal*, 1966. No. 1; and ILO: *Sharing in development . . .*, op. cit., special paper 5: "Agrarian reform".

[4] S. N. S. Cheung: "Private property rights and sharecropping", in *The Journal of Political Economy*, Nov.–Dec. 1968. See also P. K. Bardhan and T. N. Srinivasan: "Cropsharing tenancy in agriculture: A theoretical and empirical analysis", in *The American Economic Review*, Mar. 1971; and A. K. Sen: *Employment, technology and development*, op. cit., Ch. 7.

[5] A. Takahashi: *Land and peasants in Central Luzon: Socio-economic structure of a Philippine village* (Honolulu, East–West Center Press, 1970); and idem: "The peasantization of *kasamá* tenants" in F. Lynch (ed.): *View from the paddy: Empirical studies of Philippine rice farming and tenancy* (Manila, Philippine Sociological Society, 1972).

workers than farmers. He also observed that own-family workers rarely worked on their own farms, but hired themselves out to other farmers. This was due to the share-cropping arrangement whereby the landlord's share was determined by *net* farm output. Hence, to maximise household income, tenants allocated as much of their own and family labour to paid work in other farms as they could. Takahashi therefore concluded that: "The *kasamá* [share-cropper] ... was more an agricultural worker than a farmer. ... In fact, there was no clear economic and social stratification between the *kasamá* and the wage labourer, even though the latter was employed by the former. *Kasamá* and wage labourers moved from one status to the other with frequency and ease."[1] He also states: "It is a characteristic of rice-growing in the Philippines that even small farmers are heavily dependent on hired labour."[2] Moreover, in his 1972 survey of the same village, he found that in the intervening eight years a large number of share-croppers had become lease-holders and new varieties of seeds and the new agricultural technology had been introduced. These changes in the peasants' environment had led to a noticeable increase of own-family labour on the farm. They now attempted "to maximise their net returns, so that the roles of farm labourers are changing. Family labour is increasing its significance as the principal and essential element in agricultural production."[3]

It is difficult to say how far this evidence can be generalised. However, to the extent that it can, and given the earlier evidence on the similarity of productivity per hectare on farms by different tenurial groups, it would suggest that certainly on share-cropped farms, and possibly on leasehold farms too, the local agricultural wage can be taken to be a fair representation of the value marginal product of local labour. Thus Takahashi in his 1970 study explicitly states that "when householders and their family members are engaged in the work mentioned above, they pay themselves the same wages that they pay hired labourers".[4] Thus an approximate value for the output forgone by removing an agricultural worker will be given by the annual earnings of an agricultural labourer, who is employed "full time" during the agricultural season.

In its *Labor force survey* for March 1971 the Bureau of the Census and Statistics gives the weekly earnings of farm labourers who worked for 40 hours or more in the survey week as 25 pesos for male labourers and 17 pesos for female labourers. This implies annual earnings at this wage rate (assuming that 50 weeks are worked per year) of 1,250 pesos for male and 850 pesos for female labourers. For a family in which both husband and wife work, this gives annual earnings of 2,100 pesos a year. In the Bureau's *Family income and expenditures survey, 1971*, the household income of a farm labourer is given as 2,248 pesos. However, as the ILO comprehensive employment strategy mission to the Philippines in 1973 observed, this seemed high compared with the quarterly income data for a labourer in rice and maize farming, which, when adjusted to become more or less comparable with the household data, was 2,060 pesos per year.

Given the relative similarity of these alternative estimates from different sources, the figure of 2,060 pesos per year for the farm labourer's household income will be taken. The relative contribution of the male and female member of the families will be taken to be in the ratio 1:0·7, given by the relative male:female farm labourer's wages from the March 1971 *Labour force survey*. Thus the male farm worker's annual earnings are 2,060 pesos/1·7 = 1,211·76 pesos and those of the female farm worker are 848·24 pesos. On a daily basis (6-day working week and 50-week working year), the male wage rate is thus

---

[1] Takahashi: "The peasantization of *kasamá* tenants", op. cit., p. 131. The main advantage to the tenant of being a tenant rather than an agricultural worker was the relative ease in obtaining credit from the landlord. Hence he would tend to put in only as much of his own labour as would ensure his retention of the tenancy.

[2] idem: *Land and peasants in Central Luzon*, op. cit., p. 97.

[3] idem: "The peasantization of *kasamá* tenants", op. cit., p. 132.

[4] idem: *Land and peasants in Central Luzon*, op. cit., p. 61.

Table 42.   Average daily wage rates for lowland and palay farmers
(pesos at current prices)

Category of farm worker	Region[1]	1965–66	1966–67	1971–72
Ploughman	II	4·41	5·90	7·87
	III	3·95	4·80	6·04
	IV	4·43	5·03	7·74
	V	6·03	6·13	8·86
	VI	3·57	3·75	5·90
	VII	3·46	3·75	5·60
	VIII	3·20	3·10	5·71
	IX	3·56	4·00	7·33
	X	4·79	5·46	5·80
	All-Philippines	4·13	4·62	6·61
Planter	II	2·72	3·14	4·66
	III	2·54	3·58	3·28
	IV	2·96	2·98	4·10
	V	4·35	4·56	5·05
	VI	2·02	2·46	2·78
	VII	2·49	2·77	3·25
	VIII	1·90	3·06	3·10
	IX	2·62	3·06	4·37
	X	2·81	4·12	3·80
	All-Philippines	2·71	3·22	3·57
Harvester	II	2·74	2·84	4·78
	III	2·91	3·86	3·06
	IV	3·79	4·84	4·75
	V	5·76	5·13	6·43
	VI	3·72	3·78	5·98
	VII	2·89	2·93	3·82
	VIII	2·52	2·61	4·02
	IX	3·35	3·64	5·17
	X	5·12	5·35	5·01
	All-Philippines	3·56	3·52	4·89

[1] For names of regions, see table 1B.

Source: Bureau of Agricultural Economics (BAECON).

$4·039 \approx 4$ pesos and the female rate rate is $2·8$ pesos. We shall take these two estimates of agricultural wage rates as the values at market prices of output forgone (average values for the Philippines) by removing agricultural labour from farm operations throughout the year. There will obviously be variations in these values for labour in different regions, and also for farm labour which is utilised only during off-peak seasons. These values of output forgone for specific types of labour will have to be estimated for particular projects, and one such estimate for the case studies evaluated in this volume is given in Chapter 4.

Something can, however, be said about the likely regional variations in these estimates of farm labourers' wage rates and hence output forgone at market prices. Table 42 gives data on the average daily wage rate for palay farmers by region, for three different

Table 43. Relative regional real wages and shadow wage rates (SWR) for lowland palay farmers, 1961–72
(all-Philippines wage rate = 100)

Region[1] and period	Category of farm worker				Output forgone per day in "all-Philippines" market price (= 4 pesos)	Value at accounting prices of palay equivalent of output forgone in communities	SWR as % of market wage (6)÷(5)
	Ploughman	Planter	Harvester	Average			
	(1)	(2)	(3)	(4)	(5)	(6)	(7)
II							
1971–72	113·07	123·96	92·83	109·95	4·398	4·204	0·9559
Average 1961–72	105·32	97·72	76·08	93·04	3·722	3·558	0·9559
III							
1971–72	88·80	89·29	60·82	79·64	3·186	3·604	1·1312
Average 1961–72	102·34	104·58	89·49	98·80	3·952	4·470	1·1311
IV							
1971–72	103·80	101·10	85·51	96·80	3·872	3·708	0·9576
Average 1961–72	99·44	94·49	101·79	98·57	3·943	3·776	0·9576
V							
1971–1972	139·77	147·51	137·11	141·46	5·658	6·130	1·0834
Average 1961–72	139·24	149·66	148·12	145·67	5·827	6·313	1·0834
VI							
1971–72	95·16	83·02	130·37	102·85	4·114	4·612	1·1211
Average 1961–72	89·75	79·95	116·76	95·49	3·820	4·282	1·1209
VII							
1971–72	83·72	89·96	77·19	83·62	3·345	3·639	1·0879
Average 1961–72	84·66	91·20	82·25	86·04	3·442	3·745	1·0880
VIII							
1971–72	86·04	86·48	81·88	84·80	3·392	3·635	1·0716
Average 1961–72	77·14	84·16	75·87	79·06	3·162	3·389	1·0718
IX							
1971–72	106·93	118·04	101·96	108·97	4·359	4·758	1·0915
Average 1961–72	96·49	106·85	103·14	102·16	4·086	4·460	1·0915
X							
1971–72	96·43	116·97	112·58	108·66	4·346	5·018	1·1546
Average 1961–72	115·75	121·57	143·20	126·84	5·074	5·859	1·1547

[1] For names of regions, see table 1B.

categories of farm worker. In making these wage rates comparable, the differences in palay prices between the regions must be taken into account—that is, we should like to have the palay equivalent of the various regional wage rates, and this will enable us to determine the relative regional real wages of farm labourers at both market and shadow prices.

From table 30 we know the regional differences in the "farm gate" prices for palay. Taking the all-Philippines wage rate and palay prices as our benchmark, we obtain the regional real wage rates, and their percentage differences from the all-Philippines wage rate given in table 43. Using these percentage differences, we can then deduce the regional output forgone at market prices per farm worker withdrawn, given our estimate of the all-

Table 44.   Shadow wage rates (SWR) for rural labour by region
(pesos per day)

Region[1]	Competitive wage (W_f)	SWR	SWR/W_f	Market wage			
				6 pesos per day (W)		8 pesos per day (W)	
				SWR	SWR/W	SWR	SWR/W
	(1)	(2)	(3)	(4)	(5)	(6)	(7)
II	4·40	4·20	0·96	5·07	0·84	6·18	0·77
III	3·19	3·60	1·13	5·15	0·85	6·26	0·78
IV	3·87	3·71	0·96	4·94	0·82	6·11	0·76
V	5·66	6·13	1·08	6·32	1·05	7·65	0·95
VI	4·11	4·61	1·12	5·72	0·95	6·89	0·86
VII	3·35	3·64	1·09	5·21	0·86	6·45	0·80
VIII	3·39	3·64	1·07	5·09	0·84	6·22	0·77
IX	4·36	4·76	1·09	5·73	0·95	6·96	0·87
X	4·35	5·02	1·15	6·07	1·01	7·40	0·92
All-Philippines	4·00	4·25	1·08	5·63	0·93	7·02	0·87

[1] For names of regions, see table 1B.

Sources: Col. (1)—table 43, col. 5; col. (2)—table 43, col. 6; col. (3)—table 43, col. 7; cols. 4–7—computed from equation (18) in the text.

Philippine value of this magnitude of 4 pesos per day for male labourers (we disregard female labour, but estimates for regional female labour can be derived on the same principles from the data in table 43). These estimates are given in col. (5) of the table.

Furthermore, if we assume for simplicity's sake that output forgone by withdrawing farm labourers is palay, we can then use our palay accounting ratio to convert the value of output forgone at market prices into accounting prices. This is done in col. (6) of the table.

These values of output forgone at border prices give the SWR for farm labour hired at the market wages given in col. (5) of the table. Col. (7) gives the SWR as a percentage of the local wage. It will be noted that for some regions the SWR is greater than the market wage. This merely reflects the fact that for a number of regions the market price of palay is below the accounting price (see the second section of this appendix).

If, however, the labourer is hired at a higher wage rate, say W, there will be the extra cost the economy incurs by providing him with the extra consumption at market prices given by the difference between W and W_f, the competitive farm labourer's wage. This extra consumption has first to be converted into its border price equivalent value by revaluing it, using the standard consumption conversion factor for farm labour (table 1B). The extra consumption cost at border prices will therefore be $(W - W_f)/C_f$. Not the whole of this extra consumption cost is a social cost, however, for that would imply an infinite premium on savings or, in other words, that no social value was attached to increases in the current consumption of relatively poor contemporary farm workers. We therefore have to revalue this extra consumption at border prices by using the distri- butional weights (tables 34 and 35) which take account of both intertemporal and intra- temporal income distributional judgements. If this weight is d_f, then $d_f(W + W_f)/C_f$ of the extra consumption generated will be socially valuable, and hence the SWR will be

$$SWR = Y + [(W - W_f)/C_f](1 - d_f). \tag{18}$$

Table 45. Structure of earnings by industry, March 1971
(pesos per week)

Industry	Males	Females
Agriculture, forestry, fishing and hunting	*31*	*20*
Palay and maize farming	24	19
Sugar-cane farming	25	17
Tobacco farming	—	—
Abaca and other fibre farming	34	—
Coconut farming	30	—
Fruit-tree farms, vegetable root crops	34	—
Livestock and poultry farming	—	—
Agricultural services	—	—
Forestry and logging	54	—
Fishing, hunting, trapping and game propagation	31	—
Mining and quarrying	*60*	—
Coalmining and metal-mining (including crude petrol and natural gas)	65	—
Other mining and quarrying (stone quarrying, clay and sand pits, chemical and fertiliser mining, salt-mining)	49	—
Manufacturing	*64*	*37*
Electricity, gas, water and sanitary services	*69*	—
Construction	*47*	—
Road and bridge construction	52	—
Building construction	44	—
Other construction (including fishpond and unspecified)	51	—
Commerce	*68*	*38*
Wholesale trade	65	—
Sari-sari stores	—	14
Hawking and peddling	—	—
Other retail trade	48	31
Banks and other financial institutions	95	71
Insurance	106	—
Real estate	—	—
Transportation, storage and communication	*81*	*59*
Government, community, business and recreational services	*93*	*87*
Personal services	*36*	*14*
Domestic services	24	14
Other personal services	47	26
Industry not otherwise reported	*50*	—
All workers, average earnings	*62*	*44*

Source: Bureau of the Census and Statistics: *Survey of Households Bulletin—Labour Force,* Series 28, Mar. 1971, tables 47 and 49.

Table 46.   Structure of earnings by occupation, March 1971
            (pesos per week)

Occupation	Males	Females
Professional, technical	*111*	*97*
Administrative, executive and managerial	*121*	—
Clerical workers	*104*	*60*
Sales workers	*63*	*25*
Salespersons and related workers	50	22
Shop assistants and related workers	29	—
Farmers, farm labourers		
Fishermen, hunters	28	18
Farmer tenants	23	—
Farm labourers	25	17
Fishermen	29	—
Forestry workers	48	—
Miners, quarrymen, etc.	*47*	—
Workers in transportation and communication operations	*69*	—
Drivers, road transport	70	—
Conductors, rail and road	41	—
Inspectors, supervisors	85	—
Mail carriers and messengers	48	—
Craftsmen, path-process workers, etc.	*53*	*31*
Spinners, weavers, dyers	54	26
Tailors, seamstresses, etc.	40	29
Carpenters, joiners	41	—
Electricians	60	—
Painters	52	—
Bricklayers, masons, plasterers and other construction workers	42	—
Packers, labellers	33	43
Manual workers and labourers	*41*	—
In transportation, etc.	36	—
In construction	46	—
Services and related occupations	*55*	*15*
Housekeepers, cooks, maids	17	14
Washers, bar-tenders	36	20
Launderers, dry cleaners, pressers	—	17
All workers, average earnings	*62*	*44*

Source: Bureau of the Census and Statistics: *Survey of Households Bulletin—Labour Force*, Series 28, Mar. 1971, tables 47 and 49.

The values of the SWR for rural labour employed locally at a range of wage rates higher than the locally competitive farm labourer's wage, for different regions and taking account of inter-regional income distribution, are given in table 44.

Urban labour

Tables 45 and 46 give data on the weekly earnings of workers by industry and occupation for March 1971.

In determining shadow wages in the urban sector, we must first determine the wage for unskilled labour in the organised and unorganised urban sectors. Second, we have to decide whether the organised sector wage is in any sense an "institutional" wage, and hence whether the migration effects of increasing organised sector employment, analysed earlier, are likely to be of any importance for the Philippines.

We begin by making some estimates of the unorganised and organised sector wages for unskilled labour. The following table gives daily wage rates for labourers taken from several surveys, the differing coverage of which can give us a fair idea of unskilled wage rates in various parts of the urban sector.

	Central Bank (1972)	Bureau of the Census and Statistics (1971)	Government (1972)	Wage and Position Classification Office (WAPCO) (1971)	US Navy Dept. (1971)	Public corporations (SSS/GSIS) (1972)
Labourers's wage (pesos per day)	10·29	6·5	9·75	9·9	13·12	17·66

The data from the Bureau of the Census and Statistics refer to all workers; however, from table 46 it can be seen that the daily wage given by the Bureau (6·5 pesos per day) is quite close to that for manual workers, tailors, washers, bar-tenders and salespersons. This therefore probably represents a close approximation to the unorganised sector wage for unskilled labour. The Central Bank and WAPCO surveys cover large firms, and the similarity between their results and the wage in the government sector can be taken as evidence that the organised sector unskilled labourer's wage is *probably* about 9–10 pesos a day. The wage rates given in the United States Navy Department survey indicate the wage rate for unskilled labour in the foreign investment sector, whilst the SSS and GSIS data show that public corporations too are part of the really high wage end of the organised sector labour market. There would thus seem to be two organised sector wage rates for unskilled labour: about 10 pesos a day for most large-scale manufacturing and most government employment, and about 13 pesos a day for the unskilled labour élite in foreign companies and autonomous public corporations. We shall try and determine the SWR for all three types of urban unskilled wage rate for the unorganised, organised normal and organised élite groups.

The second question we have to answer is whether the organised sector wage is in any sense an institutional wage which is far above the supply price of labour to the sector. If there is to be such an institutional wage, there must clearly be some institution capable of enforcing a wage higher than the supply price of labour. There seems to be little evidence in the Philippines to suggest that there is any such enforcement agency. As in most other developing countries a minimum wage of 8 pesos a day is laid down for urban labour. However, unlike the position in most other countries there does not seem to be any attempt by the Government to enforce this minimum wage; nor are trade unions strong enough as yet to enforce an institutional wage which is much higher than the supply price of labour; nor is there any evidence in the Philippines of the excessive rural–urban migration assumed to be induced by high institutional organised sector wages in other

Asian and African countries.[1] One simple piece of evidence to support this is provided by the movement in the urban unemployment rate over the past decade. Thus from census data it appears that the urban unemployment rate fell from 12 per cent in 1960 to 9 per cent in 1970, whilst according to the Bureau of the Census and Statistics Survey of Households data the rate fell from 10·7 per cent in 1965 to 8·6 per cent in 1971. The Harris–Todaro–Harberger type of model with "wage-gap"-induced migration would, however, predict a fairly stable and probably increasing unemployment rate. Moreover, we can make a crude estimate of the number of migrants attracted to urban areas by each "extra" urban job created. For this we shall use two sets of data: data on the urban labour force pieced together by the ILO comprehensive employment strategy mission from the 1960 and 1970 censuses; and data available from the Bureau of the Census and Statistics *Labour force surveys* for 1965 and 1971. The basic data and the calculations are given in tables 47 and 48. From these it can be seen that for every extra urban job created (over and above those to meet the natural increases in the urban labour forces through population increase), there were 1·11 migrants on the ILO data and 1·03 migrants on the BCS data. The figure for Manila was slightly higher at 1·34.

From the same data we can also calculate the number of migrants per vacancy in the urban sector on Harris–Todaro–Harberger lines. If we assume that over the fairly long periods 1960–70 (from ILO data) and 1965–71 (BCS data) the probability of finding an urban sector job (P_e) was given by the ratio of the total vacancies occurring over the period (V_t) and the number of urban jobseekers (which would be the unemployed at the base date, plus new entrants through urban population increase, plus migrants), the number of migrants per increase in urban jobs (M) is simply

$$M = 1/P_e = U_t/V_t.[2]$$

From the data given in tables 41, 46 and 47, this implies the following values of P_e and M:

	P_e	M
ILO		
All-Philippines urban	0·77	1·3
Manila	0·74	1·4
BCS		
Urban	0·70	1·4

These figures are again quite close to the earlier figures we derived for the number of extra migrants per extra urban job.

Finally, we can use the formula derived in equation (17) above for an extension of the Todaro–Harberger type of migration model by relating the supply price of labour (L) to the urban sector, the number of migrants (M) and the wage differential in the urban organised (W_{mu}) and unorganised sector (W_{su}), namely

$$L = \frac{(W_{mu} - W_{su})}{M} + W_{su}.$$

From this we can derive the implicit supply price of migrants to the urban sector, given that $W_{mu} = 10$ pesos; $W_{su} = 6·5$ pesos; $M = 1·3$. By substitution in the above formula

[1] See J. R. Harris and M. P. Todaro: "Migration, unemployment and development: A two-sector analysis", in *The American Economic Review*, Mar. 1970; and A. C. Harberger: "On measuring the social opportunity cost of labour", in *International Labour Review* (Geneva), June 1971.

[2] See Lal: "Disutility of effort . . .", op. cit.

Table 47. Estimates by the ILO comprehensive employment strategy mission of rural-urban migration, 1960–70

Item	All urban		Manila	
	1960	1970	1960	1970
Population	5 640 200	8 773 600	2 007 100	3 168 100
Participation rate (percentage)	52	48	52	48[1]
Unemployment rate (percentage)	12	9	12	10·2[2]
Labour force	2 932 900	4 211 300	1 043 700	1 520 700
Unemployed	351 900	379 000	125 200	155 100
Employed	2 581 000	3 832 300	918 500	1 365 600

	Urban	Manila
Hence		
(1) Increase in labour force	1 278 400	477 000
(2) Increase in employment (V_t)	1 251 300	447 100
(3) Increase in labour force through population growth	$2\,932\,900[(1\cdot03)^{10}-1]$ $=1\,008\,900$	$1\,043\,700[(1\cdot03)^{10}-1]$ $=359\,000$
(4) Increase in labour force through migration	$1\,278\,400-1\,008\,900$ $=269\,500$	$477\,000-359\,000$ $=88\,000$
(5) Increase in employment over that provided for natural increase in urban population	$1\,251\,300-1\,008\,900$ $=242\,400$	$447\,100-359\,000$ $=88\,100$
(6) Number of migrants per "extra" job created	$269\,500/242\,400$ $=1\cdot11$	$118\,000/88\,100$ $=1\cdot34$
(7) Total number of jobseekers (U_t)	$1\,278\,400+351\,900$ $=1\,630\,300$	$477\,000+125\,200$ $=602\,200$
(8) $P_e = V_t/U_t$	$1\,251\,300/1\,630\,300$ $=0\cdot77$	$447\,100/602\,200$ $=0\cdot74$
(9) $M = 1/P_e$	$1\cdot299 \approx 1\cdot3$	$1\cdot351 \approx 1\cdot4$

[1] Assumed to be the same as for all urban.   [2] From Bureau of the Census and Statistics: *Labour force survey*, Mar. 1971.

this yields $L = 9$ pesos. How plausible is this value for L? We have determined that the likely average rural wage is about 4 pesos a day. The likely rural–urban price differential is about 25 per cent.[1] This means that, at urban prices, income forgone for the rural migrant will be $(4 \times 1\cdot25) = 6$ pesos a day. The remaining 3 pesos could well be a reasonable estimate of the costs of migration (transport, etc.), including the psychic costs.

Furthermore, studies on the characteristics of migrants[2] show that migrants to Manila come from rural towns rather than villages. There thus seems to be a two-stage migration procedure—from the villages to the rural towns, and from the latter to Manila. More-

[1] The ILO comprehensive employment strategy mission estimated that the average price difference between Manila and other urban sectors was about 26 per cent: that is, if an "other urban" family were to spend the same share of its budget on non-food, non-housing and similar items, it would need an income some 26 per cent higher.

[2] See discussion in M. Mangahas: *A broad view of the Philippine employment problem*, Discussion paper no. 72–76, 4 Dec. 1972 (Manila, University of the Philippines, School of Economics, Institute of Economic Development and Research).

Table 48. Estimates by the Bureau of the Census and Statistics[1] of rural-urban migration, 1965–71

Item	1965	1971
Urban labour force	3 313 000	4 157 000
Unemployment	355 000	360 000
Unemployment rate (percentage)	10·7	8·6
Employed	2 958 000	3 797 000

Hence

(1) Increase in labour force	844 000
(2) Increase in employment (V_t)	839 000
(3) Increase in labour force through population growth	$3\ 313\ 000[(1 \cdot 03)^6 - 1] = 642\ 700$
(4) Increase in labour force through migration	$844\ 000 - 642\ 700 = 201\ 300$
(5) Increase in employment over that provided for natural increase in urban population	$839\ 000 = 642\ 700 = 196\ 300$
(6) Number of migrants per "extra" job created	$201\ 300/196\ 300 = 1 \cdot 03$
(7) Total number of jobseekers (U_t)	$844\ 000 + 355\ 000 = 1\ 199\ 000$
(8) $P_e = V_t/U_t$	$839\ 000/1\ 199\ 000 = 0 \cdot 70$
(9) $M = 1/P_e$	$1 \cdot 429 \approx 1 \cdot 4$

[1] Labour force surveys.

over, "four out of ten [migrants to Manila] found first jobs within a week, three out of ten needed up to a month, and one out of ten needed up to six months".[1]

All this evidence seems to suggest the following conclusions: (a) there is a spectrum of urban wage rates, with those for unskilled labour being slightly lower on average for those in the unorganised urban services sector as compared with organised large-scale manufacturing (the differentials are probably accounted for by the need for more regulated machine-paced work in manufacturing, as well as the possibility that employers pay a wage which may be slightly higher than the supply price of labour to ensure a more stable labour force); (b) there is not much evidence of an urban wage gap determined by a high institutional wage; (c) an exception to (b) is, however, provided by the small foreign investment sector. Even in this sector, however, since much foreign investment is concentrated on the extractive industries, the 13·12 pesos paid per day (according to the United States Navy Department survey) is not very much more than the 11 pesos per day which, according to the Bureau of the Census and Statistics Survey of Households, is received on average by coalminers and metal-miners (table 45). Furthermore, this high wage sector is not likely to be very large,[2] and it is by no means clear that its wage rates have either a demonstration effect on other urban sector wages and/or enter directly into the calculations of the average rural–urban migrant.

Hence, in order to determine shadow wages in the urban sector in the Philippines, we shall make the following assumptions:

(a) the unorganised sector wage is 6·50 pesos per day;
(b) the organised normal sector wage is 10 pesos per day;

---

[1] Mangahas, op. cit., p. 6.

[2] The ILO comprehensive employment strategy mission estimated that it probably employs 40,000–80,000 workers. It also argued that it has a serious impact on the over-all earnings structure. However, in the absence of any time-series data on relative movements in wage rates between this and other sectors, this conclusion is open to doubt.

(c) the organised élite sector wage is 13 pesos per day;

(d) on average there are 1·3 rural migrants per net increase in organised urban sector jobs:[1]

(e) there is a process of substitution whereby organised sector jobs are at the margin filled by former unorganised sector employees, and the latter are replaced by rural migrants (though later we take account of the effects of bidding up wages).

The SWR for unskilled labour in the three urban categories may therefore be derived as follows.

Unorganised

An extra unorganised sector job will, on our above argument, ultimately result in a rural worker migrating. The average output forgone (according to our earlier argument) for a rural worker will be 4 pesos of palay at market prices. Its value at "all-Philippines" accounting prices is $4/0·937 = 4·27$ pesos. We next estimate the resource cost of providing the worker with extra consumption of $(6·5 − 4) = 2·5$ pesos.[2] Using our consumption conversion factor for urban household incomes of 3,000–3,900 pesos, i.e. 1·23 (table 1B), we get the accounting value of this cost of extra consumption as 2·03 pesos. Not all of this, however, is a social cost for distributional reasons. Using the distributional weight (d derived from table 34) for households with an annual income of 408·17 pesos per head, of 0·2477 (assuming $e = 2$), we get the net social cost of the extra 2·03 pesos of consumption at accounting prices of $[2·03(1 − 0·2477)] = 1·53$ pesos. Hence the shadow wage for unorganised sector unskilled labour is

$$(4·27 + 1·53) = 5·8 \text{ pesos}$$

or

$$SWR = (5·8/6·5)W_{su} = 0·9W_{su}.$$

Organised normal

The organised normal sector wage is 10 pesos. The SWR for organised normal sector employees (ignoring rural–urban migration) will be:

(a) the social cost of employing a worker, assuming he had been hired at the unorganised sector wage of 6·5 pesos: this is just $SWR_{su} = 0·9W_{su} = 5·8$ pesos; *plus*

(b) the resource cost at accounting prices of hiring the workers at the higher organised sector wage of 10 pesos. At market prices this resource cost is $(10 − 6·5) = 3·5$ pesos. The consumption conversion factor we use is again for 3,000–3,900 pesos, i.e. 1·23. This yields the resource cost at accounting prices of $(3·5/1·23) = 2·85$ pesos; *less*

(c) the social benefit of providing poor workers with extra consumption. For this we take from table 34 the distributional weight for the income class of 481 pesos per head (0·1779) to get $0·1779 × 2·85$ pesos.

---

[1] Thus we assume that the increase in unorganised sector jobs takes account of the natural increase in the labour force through population increases, leaving the organised sector to provide the extra jobs in the urban sector which attract the migrants. Thus the annual surveys of industrial data show that the employment in large-scale manufacturing increased by 163,398 between 1959 and 1969. According to the data in table 47, and our derivations therein, the number of extra jobs created between 1960 and 1970 was 196,300. So the above assumption may be approximately correct.

[2] Strictly speaking, we ought to take account of savings and taxes. However, from household survey data it appears that nothing is saved at this level of income, and taxes are an extremely small proportion of total expenditure.

Table 49. Summary of accounting wages for urban unskilled labour: market wage (W), shadow wage (SWR) and SWR/W per day (assuming $e = 2$)

Sector	W	SWR	SWR/W
Unorganised			
Drawn from rural sector	6·5	5·8	0·9
From bidding up wages within the sector	6·5	5·1	0·8
Organised normal			
Drawn from unorganised sector	10·0	7·15	0·7
Taking account of rural–urban migration	10·0	8·43	0·8
From bidding up wages within the sector	10·0	6·06	0·6
Organised élite			
Drawn from organised normal sector	13·0	11·09	0·9
From bidding up wages within the sector	13·0	9·37	0·7

The SWR is then

$$\text{SWR}_{mu} = 5 \cdot 8 + 2 \cdot 85 \, (1 - 0 \cdot 1779)$$
$$= 5 \cdot 8 + 2 \cdot 35$$
$$= 7 \cdot 15 \text{ pesos}$$

or

$$\text{SWR}_{mu} = 7 \cdot 15/10$$
$$= 0 \cdot 72 \; W_{mu}.$$

If we take account of rural–urban migration, then (from our earlier discussion) 1·3 rural migrants will move to the cities. The output forgone in the above derivation has therefore been understated by the output forgone at accounting prices of 0·3 rural workers. Given that for one rural worker the accounting value of output forgone is 4·27 pesos, for 0·3 workers it will be $4 \cdot 27 \times 0 \cdot 3 = 1 \cdot 28$ pesos. Adding this to the SWR estimated above—which did not take account of rural–urban migration—we get the final value of the SWR as

$$\text{SWR}_{mu} = (7 \cdot 15 + 1 \cdot 28) \text{ pesos}$$
$$= 8 \cdot 43 \text{ pesos}$$

or

$$\text{SWR}_{mu} = 8 \cdot 43/10$$
$$= 0 \cdot 84 \; W_{mu}.$$

Organised élite

The SWR derivation for this group is now straightforward, given our assumption that workers hired by this sector came from the organised normal sector. We have calculated output forgone at accounting prices as $\text{SWR}_{mu} = 8 \cdot 43$ pesos (which includes the rural–urban migration costs). Adding the net costs of the extra consumption expenditure due to paying the higher wage of 13 pesos,

$$(13 - 10)(1 - d_{oe}) = 3(1 - 0 \cdot 1143) \text{ pesos}$$

(assuming d_{oe} is the distributional weight corresponding to the income class of 600 pesos per head), we obtain

$$\text{SWR}_{eu} = (8 \cdot 43 + 2 \cdot 66)$$
$$= 11 \cdot 09 \text{ pesos};$$

or

$$SWR_{eu} = 11 \cdot 09/13$$
$$= 0 \cdot 85\, W_{eu}.$$

All these estimates are based on the assumption that distributional weights for $e = 2$ are valid. These estimates are summarised in table 49.

Furthermore, given our earlier argument about skilled labour within each of the three sectors, we can use the formula derived earlier to obtain the shadow wages of skilled labour. Thus, on our earlier argument, the SWR for skilled labour of type b in sector j will be

$$SWR_{bj} = [(W_{sj} - W_{uj})/A_j] + SWR_{uj}$$

where

W_{sj} = nominal wage of the particular type of skilled labour in sector j;
W_{uj} = nominal unskilled wage in the sector;
SWR_{uj} = shadow wage of labour in the sector; and
A_j = accounting ratio for the output of the sector.

If W is the ratio of SWR_{uj}/W_{uj}, then

$$SWR_{sj} = \frac{W_{sj}}{A_j} - \left(\frac{1}{A_j} - W\right) W_{uj}.$$

From this the shadow wage of semi-skilled labour in our three sectors is:

(a) unorganised:

$$SWR_{ss} = [(W_{ss} - W_{su})/A_s] + (0 \cdot 9 \times 6 \cdot 5).$$

Taking A_s for traditional services as equal to $1 \cdot 16$ (table 1A), we obtain:[1]

$$SWR_{ss} = 0 \cdot 86\, W_{su} + 0 \cdot 25;$$

(b) organised normal:

$$SWR_{son} = (W_{son} - W_{mu})/A_m + (0 \cdot 84)10.$$

Taking A_m as $1 \cdot 2$ (i.e. between the ratios for modern consumer goods and modern capital goods from table 1A), we obtain:

$$SWR_{son} = 0 \cdot 8\, W_{son} + 0 \cdot 07;$$

(c) organised élite:

$$SWR_{soe} = (W_{soe} - W_{eu})/A_e + (0 \cdot 85)13.$$

Taking A_e for modern capital goods as equal to $1 \cdot 25$ (table 1A), we obtain:

$$SWR_{soe} = 0 \cdot 8\, W_{soe} + 0 \cdot 65.$$

The final complication concerns the effects on the SWR of any bidding up of wages in the sector where employment is being offered. We have derived the SWR for these cases in equation (16) above. The first part of the equation gives the SWR for the proportion of labour which is drawn conventionally from the other sectors. The second part requires estimates of:

E_j (wage elasticity of demand for labour in sector j);
d_{wj}/d_{ej} (distributional weight for workers/employers in sector j); and
c_{wj}/c_{ej} (consumption propensities of workers and employers in sector j).

---

[1] Note that in the following derivations we have used the following values: $W_{su} = 6 \cdot 5$; $W_{mu} = 10$; $W_{eu} = 13$; and that $0 \cdot 9$, $0 \cdot 84$ and $0 \cdot 85$ are the values of the respective shadow to nominal wages of the three types of unskilled labour (that is SWR_{ku}/W_{ku}, with $k = s, m, e$).

Table 50.   Average savings per worker by income class, rural and urban, 1957, 1965 and 1971

Income class (pesos per year)	Rural		Urban	
	Amount (pesos)	Percentage of income	Amount (pesos)	Percentage of income
1957				
Under 250	−30	−24·0	−76	−55·5
250–499	−23	−10·8	−56	−23·3
500–749	0	0·0	−22	−6·0
750–999	27	6·9	8	1·7
1 000–1 499	74	14·1	29	4·2
1 500–1 999	130	17·4	107	10·5
2 000–2 999	506	54·5	158	11·7
3 000–4 999	411	27·8	256	13·5
5 000+	1 147	40·2	832	19·3
1965				
Under 500	−401	−251·1	−640	−352·1
500–999	−342	−100·1	−538	−126·0
1 000–1 499	−289	−51·4	−528	−76·6
1 500–1 999	−189	−24·2	−464	−45·3
2 000–2 499	−123	−12·6	−466	−35·1
2 500–2 999	3	0·3	−423	−28·0
3 000–3 999	5	0·4	−370	−21·4
4 000–4 999	245	15·0	−303	−15·7
5 000–5 999	227	12·7	−212	−8·9
6 000–7 999	791	32·7	−60	−2·3
8 000–9 999	1 018	35·2	−317	10·0
10 000+	980	34·7	1 965	25·5
1971				
Under 500	−1 151	−371·3	−1 462	−527·2
500–999	−1 025	−162·9	−1 260	−204·1
1 000–1 499	−966	−92·9	−1 166	−120·5
1 500–1 999	−903	−62·4	−1 483	−100·8
2 000–2 499	−761	−44·2	−1 226	−64·8
2 500–2 999	−662	−31·4	−1 049	−49·6
3 000–3 999	−340	−0·3	−1 169	−44·0
4 000–4 999	−199	−6·7	−997	−31·3
5 000–5 999	−8	−2·8	−818	−25·6
6 000–7 999	170	5·2	−787	−19·5
8 000–9 999	411	9·2	−466	−9·9
10 000–14 999	1 217	22·7	−341	−5·4
15 000–19 999	2 155	24·5	95	1·2
20 000+	7 844	55·6	6 063	34·5

Source: Bureau of the Census and Statistics: *Family income and expenditures surveys.*

Table 51. Average savings per family by income class, rural and urban, 1961

Income class (pesos per year)	Rural		Urban	
	Amount (pesos)	Percentage of income	Amount (pesos)	Percentage of income
1961				
Under 500	−360	−100·8	−367	−106·4
500–999	−294	−40·0	−352	−47·5
1 000–1 499	−202	−16·5	−321	−25·6
1 500–1 999	−1	−0·1	−233	−13·5
2 000–2 499	237	10·7	−66	−3·0
2 500–2 999	378	13·9	202	7·4
3 000–3 999	772	22·7	327	9·5
4 000–4 999	1 174	26·3	341	7·7
5 000–5 999	1 601	29·1	454	8·2
6 000–7 999	1 220	18·2	588	8·6
8 000–9 999	2 899	33·3	1 711	19·2
10 000+	6 120	43·6	8 644	43·5

Source: Bureau of the Census and Statistics: *Family income and expenditures surveys.*

The annex to this section derives estimates of the wage elasticity of demand for large-scale manufacturing, modern services, traditional services and agriculture. The SWR of the portion of the incremental labour force in sector j drawn from that sector (ΔL_j) is given (see equation (16)) by

$$\text{SWR}_{\Delta Lj} = \Delta L_j W_j \left[\frac{1}{A_j} - \frac{1}{E_j} (d_{wj} c_{wj} - d_{ej} c_{ej}) \right].$$

For our three urban sectors and the rural sector we have the following values for the variables for unskilled labour and the computed SWR_{Lj} (assuming $\Delta L_j = 1$).

	W_j	A_j	E_j	d_{wj}[1]	d_{ej}[1]	c_{wj}	c_{ej}	$\text{SWR}_{\Delta Lj}$
Unorganised	6·5	1·18[2]	2·0	0·1779	0·0411	1·00	0·94	5·046
Organised normal	10·0	1·40[3]	1·4	0·1779	0·0340	1·00	0·93	6·057
Organised élite	13·0	1·25	1·1	0·1143	0·0147	0·96	0·91	9·367
Rural	4·0	0·94	1·1	0·2471	0·0411	1·00	0·94	3·483

The values for c_{wj} and c_{ej} have been derived from the data on savings rates by income group given in tables 50 and 51. From these it appears that (assuming that an average household has six members), none of the goups we are considering saved anything in

---

[1] The weights are for $e = 2$ for the workers in the unorganised and organised normal sectors. The weights for an average annual income per head of 481 pesos have been taken. For the organised élite sector the weights for an annual income of 600 pesos have been used. For employers the respective income categories taken for the distributional weights are: unorganised, 1,000 pesos; organised normal, 1,200 pesos; organised élite, 1,670 pesos; and rural, 1,000 pesos.

[2] Assumed to be traditional services.

[3] Assumed to be modern services.

Table 52.   Unemployment rate and labour force in agriculture by region, 1971
(percentage)

Region[1]	Unemployment rate	Labour force in agriculture
I	11·2	0·7
II	1·7	64·2
III	2·7	73·0
IV	6·3	43·3
V	8·5	37·9
VI	1·4	58·0
VII	3·4	57·4
VIII	5·2	56·6
IX	3·3	64·3
X	1·1	65·5
All Philippines	*4·8*	*51·2*

[1] For names of regions, see table 1B.

Source: Bureau of the Census and Statistics: *Labour force survey*, May 1971.

1971. However, the higher income groups (that is, those with incomes above 2,000 pesos) had to pay income taxes. Taking the latter into account, we obtain the approximate values of c for workers and employers given above and the resulting SWRs, if the increased demand for labour is met *entirely from within the sector* by bidding up wages.

Table 49 summarised the estimates of accounting wage rates for urban unskilled labour. It may appear surprising that the SWR is lower for labour drawn entirely from within a sector by bidding up the sector's wage rate. This is essentially due to the distributional shift of income from employers to workers that this process entails, and the relatively higher weight placed on increases in workers' income compared with decreases in that of employers. These favourable distributional income changes will be relatively larger when labour comes from within rather than from outside the sector. In practice, of course, as equation (16) makes clear, the increased demand for labour will be most likely met from both within and outside the sector; and to the extent that the latter's SWR is higher than the former, the SWR given by equation (16) will be higher than those computed on the assumption that labour is drawn entirely from within the sector. Finally, table 52 summarises the data on unemployment rates and the labour force in agriculture by region.

Annex: Structure of demand elasticities for labour with respect to the wage rate[1]

Summary of findings

Although only very limited and sketchy data are available, some assessment of the demand elasticities for labour with respect to the real wage rate can be made with a degree of confidence. These estimates are briefly summarised in table 53. Because of data and time constraints it has not been possible to calculate standard errors.

[1] This annex was prepared by Calje Falcke.

Table 53.   Demand elasticities for labour with respect to the real wage rate

Sector	Short run	Long run
Large manufacturing	−0·3	−1·1
Modern services	−0·4	−1·4
Traditional services	−0·5	−2·0
Agriculture	(−0·1)	−1·1

Elasticity of substitution between labour and capital

Williamson has estimated a CES production function for the Philippines.[1] Solving this function for labour, and assuming that the speed of adjustment in the long run is unity, gives the following values for the elasticity of substitution between capital and labour (strictly $\partial \ln L / \partial \ln (C/W)$ where C = rental on capital, W = real wage and L = quantity of labour):

$$\sigma = \begin{cases} 0 \cdot 24 \text{ in the short run (SR)} \\ 0 \cdot 90 \text{ in the long run (LR).} \end{cases}$$

Scott[2] gives the demand elasticity of labour with respect to wage rate as

$$\epsilon = - \frac{\sigma}{1 - w}$$

where w = share of wages in output (assuming that labour is paid its marginal product).
Taking net value added to equal total output, we have the following estimate of w:

$$w = \text{real wages/real value added.}$$

Thus an estimate of the elasticity of substitution between labour and capital, and some time-series or other data on wages and value added, will give us the required elasticity of the demand for labour.

Large manufacturing

In all manufacturing firms employing 20 or more workers, w has steadily declined from 0·28 in 1956 to 0·22 in 1961.[3] Thus, using the above values for the elasticity of substitution, and $w = 0 \cdot 22$, we have

$$\varepsilon = \begin{cases} -0 \cdot 31 \text{ in the short run} \\ -1 \cdot 15 \text{ in the long run.} \end{cases}$$

Services

The available value added and total wage bill figures are not consistent for the service sector. Instead we shall use the 1965 input/output table which gives, for wages/value added, a value of 0·34 for so-called modern services and 0·28 for traditional services. Lal[4] has estimated the ratio of payments for self-employment to value added in the two

---

[1] J. G. Williamson: "Capital accumulation, labor saving and labor absorption once more", in *The Quarterly Journal of Economics*, Feb. 1971.

[2] M. FG. Scott: *Estimates of shadow wages in Kenya* (Oxford, Nuffield College, Feb. 1973; mimeographed), p. 69.

[3] Bureau of the Census and Statistics: *Annual survey of manufactures, 1969*, table 2.

[4] See table 23.

subsectors as $0 \cdot 02$ and $0 \cdot 27$ respectively. Adding the wages and salaries ratios then gives the following estimates of w and ϵ:

$$\text{Modern services} \qquad w = 0 \cdot 36 \Rightarrow \epsilon = \begin{cases} -0 \cdot 37 \text{ in the short run} \\ -1 \cdot 41 \text{ in the long run} \end{cases}$$

$$\text{Traditional services} \qquad w = 0 \cdot 55 \Rightarrow \epsilon = \begin{cases} -0 \cdot 53 \text{ in the short run} \\ -2 \cdot 00 \text{ in the long run.} \end{cases}$$

Agriculture

For the agricultural sector the elasticity of substitution between labour and capital obtained from Williamson's CES function can presumably not be used. To obtain a new estimate, consider the definition of the elasticity of substitution

$$\eta = \frac{\dfrac{Q_K}{dQ_L}}{\dfrac{Q_K}{Q_L}} \Big/ \frac{\dfrac{P_K}{dP_L}}{\dfrac{P_K}{P_L}}$$

where

$Q =$ quantity;
$P =$ price (wage rate);
$K =$ capital; and
$L =$ labour.

In agriculture the capital consists mainly of land. If we now choose our units so that $Q_K = Q_L$ in both agriculture and manufacturing, it is likely that the numerator in the above definition is slightly larger in manufacturing than in agriculture because of the more rapid process of industrialisation in the manufacturing sector. Denote the numerators in the two cases by N_M and N_A respectively, and let us assume that $N_A = 0 \cdot 9 \, N_M$.

From the *Annual survey of manufactures, 1969*, we find that over the period 1962–69 N_M was approximately $0 \cdot 125$. Thus, N_A is taken to be in the neighbourhood of $0 \cdot 112$. Furthermore, for the denominator in the case of agriculture we find a value of $0 \cdot 152$ by using changes in the value of agricultural output per hectare (from the *Philippine yearbook of statistics, 1969*) as a proxy for changes in the price of agricultural capital, and real wages for farm labourers. Together these figures would then indicate an elasticity of substitution between labour and capital in agriculture of around $0 \cdot 7$, which seems plausible, given the elasticity of $0 \cdot 9$ in manufacturing.

Cristina Crisostomo[1] gives the equivalent man-days in agriculture. Increasing these by the proportion of self-employed ($53 \cdot 5$ per cent in 1971) and multiplying by the real wage for farm labour we get the annual real wage bill. Comparing real value added then gives an estimate of w of around $0 \cdot 35$ in both 1972 and 1971. Substituting into Scott's formula gives $\epsilon = -1 \cdot 08$ in the long run (presumably). We also note that Mangahas and Encarnacion[2] have obtained from a linear regression model the elasticity at the mean of

---

[1] Cristina Crisostomo: *Sources of output and productivity growth in the postwar Philippine agriculture*, unpublished MA thesis.

[2] M. Mangahas and J. Encarnacion, Jr.: "Production submodel of the Philippine economy, 1950–69", in National Economic and Development Authority: *Econometric models of the Philippines* (Manila, 1972).

Table 54. Shadow prices of equipment (pesos)

Type of equipment	Lifetime (years) (T)	Average annual machine-hours (H)	c.i.f. price	Port handling and other fees × 0.8144	Total capital cost at accounting prices p_e^a	% of capital cost	Annual cost of maintenance (M)		Annual cost		Fuel, lubricating grease per hour	Total daily shadow rental rate (R)		Market rental rate
							M_1	M_2	$Y_1 + M_1$	$Y_2 + M_2$		Lower bounds	Upper bounds	
		(2)	(3)	(4)	(5)	(6)	(7)		(8)	(9)	(10)	(11)	(12)	(13)
(1)														
Bulldozer D6	5–8	2 000–1 000	250 650	25 470	276 120	20–12	55 224	33 134	115 197	79 412	4·0	496·0	664·0	592·0
Bulldozer D8	5–8	,,	549 950	55 431	605 381	20–12	121 076	72 645	252 565	174 107	8·1	1 073·0	1 457·0	1 145·0
Payloader, 1·5 m⁵	5–8	,,	164 570	16 739	181 309	20–12·5	36 262	22 660	75 642	53 047	4·0	328·0	456·0	413·0
Grader	5–8	,,	220 720	22 324	243 044	23·2–14·3	56 386	34 860	109 172	75 594	4·0	464·0	640·0	426·0
Pneumatic roller	5–8	,,	103 850	11 139	114 989	20–12·5	22 999	14 374	47 975	33 646	2·3	202·0	290·0	323·0
Road roller	5–8	,,	125 590	13 091	138 681	20–12·5	27 736	17 335	57 858	40 578	2·3	242·0	346·0	258·0
Truck, 8 tons	5–7	,,	78 000	7 696	85 696	16–10	13 710	8 570	32 323	23 970	1·4	139·0	203·0	184·0
Water tank, 6 m³	5–7	,,	120 000	11 605	134 250	16–10	21 480	13 425	50 639	37 550	1·4	211·0	315·0	201·0
Farm tractor, 60 hp	5–7	,,	75 900	7 659	83 559	16–10	13 559	8 360	31 519	23 376	1·4	131·0	195·0	144·0
Crane, 15 tons	5–8	,,	242 000	24 432	266 432	12–7	31 970	18 650	89 839	63 304	3·3	386·0	538·0	639·0
Diesel hammer	5–8	,,	147 640	15 409	163 049	10–6	16 300	10 800	48 192	36 562	0·9	199·0	303·0	176·0
Air compressor, 370 cfm	4–5	,,	33 100	3 950	37 050	12·5–10	4 630	3 700	13 807	11 747	2·0	72·0	112·0	125·0
Concrete mixer, 4/50C	5–8	,,	16 616	2 020	18 636	10·5–6·5	1 957	1 210	6 005	4 333	0·5	28·0	44·0	101·0
Vibrator, 7 hp	5–8	,,	4 032	568	4 600	8–5	368	230	1 368	1 000	0·3	7·0	12·0	13·0
Concreter	5–8	,,	138 400	15 636	154 036	7·5–4·5	11 553	7 086	45 010	32 902	0·9	191·0	271·0	401·0

Note: Y_n is derived from the formula $Y_n = p_e^a \left. T_n \middle/ \displaystyle\sum_{t=0}^{T_n} \frac{1}{(1+ARI)} T_t \right.$, where T_n corresponds to the two limiting assumptions made about the lifetime of the equipment.

agricultural employment N with respect to the real agricultural wage W, i.e.

$$\frac{\Delta N}{\Delta \overline{W}} \cdot \frac{\overline{W}}{\overline{N}}$$

$\dfrac{\Delta N}{\Delta \overline{W}}$ is the regression coefficient corresponding to W, and $\overline{W}$ and $\overline{N}$ are the means.

Using time-series data from the national accounts over the period 1956–68, they obtain $\epsilon = 0.12$, which presumably is for the short run. The absolute value, 0.12, however, appears to be too low. This might be due to a slight specification error (mainly linearity) in the regression model. We also note that Mangahas and Encarnacion did not obtain significant regression coefficients for either wages or real wages in their linear recursive employment equations for the manufacturing and services sectors.

The elasticity of real value added per employee with respect to real wage rate

An attempt to estimate the demand elasticity for labour (w.r.t. wage rate) directly was made by estimating a constant elasticity model of the type

$$V = aw^b$$

where
V = real value added per employed person; and
w = real wage rate as before.

Taking logs, and differentiating, we have

$$b = \frac{\partial \log V}{\partial \log w}.$$

Hence b is an estimate of ϵ if the change in value added per employed person equals (or closely approximates) the change in the demand for labour. This could be so if the employers tend to hire more labour when the workers' average productivity goes up. However, one could equally easily argue the exact opposite: the demand for labour goes down when the average productivity per worker increases. Moreover, in the first case, because of money illusion, V tends to underestimate the true demand for labour when wages are high and overestimates the demand when wages are low. Hence b would be a downward-biased estimate of ϵ, and should at most be regarded as a lower limit of an estimate of ϵ.

Nevertheless, regressions of the above type were fitted to time-series data for large manufacturing, commerce, and agriculture. The results were far from satisfactory, one of the reasons surely being data inconsistencies. The only result that made some sort of sense was the one for agriculture which, for the period 1957–72, was in estimated form

$$\log V = 4.51 - 0.47 \log w \qquad R^2 = 0.661.$$
$$(0.10)$$

Thus the lower limit for the absolute value of the demand elasticity for labour with respect to wages is taken to be 0.5.

SHADOW RENTALS OF EQUIPMENT

In Chapter 4 we outlined the general principles on which the shadow rental on various machines can be calculated.

First, the total accounting cost of a machine is derived from the c.i.f. price plus the accounting cost of port handling and other fees at accounting prices (the latter being given by dividing the market costs of port handling, etc., by the accounting ratio for wholesale trade, $1 \cdot 23$ (see table 1A)). This yields the figures in cols. (3), (4) and (5) in table 54. Let

F	= fuel costs (given in col. (10));
A_f	= accounting ratio for petroleum and coal ($1 \cdot 14$ from table 1A);
T	= lifetime of a new machine;
H	= average annual machine-hours of service the new machine can provide;
M	= annual repair and maintenance costs;
A_m	= accounting ratio for maintenance and repairs;
ARI	= accounting rate of interest;
P_e^a	= accounting price of the machine when new; and
R	= hourly shadow rental rate of the machine.

We can then estimate R from

$$P_e^a = \sum_{t=0}^{T} H[R - (F/A_f) - (M/A_m)]/(1 + \text{ARI})^t.$$

In table 54 the accounting costs of maintenance and repairs for each machine were estimated by the engineers as a percentage of the border price of the equipment (i.e. it represented (M/A_m)). As they were uncertain about this item and the lifetime of the machines, they placed lower and upper bounds on their estimates, which together yield the estimates of the shadow rental rates on the two assumptions and in cols. (11) and (12). For comparison, the market rental rate for the equipment is given in col. (13).

MARKET AND SOCIAL PROFITABILITY
OF ALTERNATIVE TECHNIQUES

D

Given the estimates of the productivity of men and machines assembled in Appendix B and the shadow prices in Appendix C, we can now determine the relative profitability of the alternatives at market and shadow prices.

Tables 55 and 56 give the results with the *ex ante* and the revised estimates for the Capas–Botolan road. Both compare the capital-intensive and modified labour-intensive methods, and show that the latter are less costly on both sets of estimates at both sets of shadow prices as well as at market prices. The purely labour-intensive method was not in fact implemented, and hence there is no revised estimate for this. On the *ex ante* estimates the pure labour-intensive method was again superior to the capital-intensive method at all sets of prices and superior to the modified labour-intensive alternative at shadow but not at market prices.

Table 57 provides the *ex ante* and revised estimates of the market and social profitability of the modified labour-intensive and capital-intensive alternatives for building an average gravel road in the Philippines. Once again the labour-intensive alternative is cheaper at both market and shadow prices.

Table 58 shows the relative profitability of the alternative techniques for the concrete paving of roads. It shows that labour-intensive methods are profitable only on the low wage–high rental assumption, with the capital-intensive methods being cheaper both at market prices and on the high wage–low rental assumption.

Figures 18 to 20 show the costs of excavating and hauling fill material for the alternative methods at shadow prices. The results at market prices were summarised in Appendix B. Table 59 shows the haul distances at which each method of transport is socially least costly at the two limiting sets of shadow prices.

Table 55. Costs of alternative techniques for building the Capas–Botolan road at market and shadow prices (*ex ante* estimates) (pesos)

Item						Market price	Shadow price	
Code no.	Description	Quantity	Method[1]	Man-days (M) Equipment (E)			Low wage–high rental	High wage–low rental
100	Clearing and grubbing	22 ha	1	M: 5 256		43 704	20 016	37 620
				E: bullcarts and tools		7 050	4 370	4 370
			2	M: 615		6 238	3 178	5 308
				E: bulldozers and trucks		51 912	49 437	36 237
			3	M: 1 074		9 112	4 311	7 800
				E: bulldozer and handtools		37 426	45 291	33 695
105a	Excavation (average) 100 m haul)	160 000 m³	1 and 3	M: 57 696		569 784	245 703	503 434
				E: bullcarts, wheelbarrows, ploughs and pneumatic roller		246 216	165 715	140 371
			2	M: 2 226		22 505	19 397	20 821
				E: bulldozers, graders, sheepfoot and pneumatic rollers		940 829	1 141 653	836 732
105b	Soft rock excavation	2 982 m³	1	M: 5 160		42 246	78 440	36 480
				E: handtools and wheelbarrows		3 080	2 957	2 957
			2	M: 289		4 839	3 046	3 632
				E: dynamite and bulldozer		49 558	41 384	31 590
			3	M: 2 442		21 409	10 491	18 521
				E: dynamite and wheelbarrow		24 006	20 938	19 618
106	Excavation for structures	790 m³	1	M: 725		6 352	2 975	5 225
				E: handtools from item 105a		0	0	0
			2	M: 651		6 320	2 620	5 443
				E: handtools from item 105a		0	0	0
			3	M: 651		5 332	2 281	4 612
				E: handtools from item 105a		0	0	0

Item	Description	Quantity	Method	Input			
110	Foundation fill	125 m³	1	M: 36	300	044	258
				E: dump-trucks and payloader	750	638	638
			2	M: 55	458	197	384
				E: dump-trucks and payloader	798	492	347
			3	M: 58	480	195	425
				E: farm tractor and trailers	567	695	467
111	Overhaul	143 000 station meter	1	M: 900	7 200	2 880	6 300
				E: bullcarts	7 200	3 915	3 915
			2	M: 45	540	432	432
				E: dump-trucks and payloaders	19 830	12 930	9 090
			3	M: 74	740	473	614
				E: farm tractor and trailers	7 602	9 983	6 706
200	Borrow base (5 km)	11 100 m³	1	M: 3 005	25 992	13 480	22 580
				E: dump-trucks and payloader	89 163	37 308	35 108
			2	M: 329	3 651	2 480	2 817
				E: dump-trucks and payloader	88 260	67 904	47 877
			3	M: 4 330	37 896	18 810	41 000
				E: farm tractor and trailers	68 506	71 046	48 600
405	Concrete	381 m³	1, 2 and 3	M: 1 308	13 100	2 823	10 870
			1, 2 and 3	E: concrete mixer	11 416	14 096	9 350
406	Reinforcing steel	34.5 tons	1, 2 and 3	M: 412	3 600	1 680	2 610
			1, 2 and 3	E: iron cutter and bender	290	278	278
505	Reinforced concrete pipes	645 m	1, 2 and 3	M: 3 656	32 860	18 348	27 708
			1, 2 and 3	E: handtools			
			1, 2 and 3	Materials: concrete and steel bar	172 014	146 682	146 682
Total cost (Cost per km)			1	Equipment, materials and labour	1 282 317 (222 624)	706 448 (122 647)	996 754 (173 048)
			2	Equipment, materials and labour	1 429 018 (248 093)	1 533 057 (266 156)	1 198 208 (208 022)
			3	Equipment, materials and labour	1 262 359 (219 160)	783 839 (136 083)	1 023 361 (177 667)

¹ Methods: 1 = labour-intensive; 2 = capital-intensive; 3 = modified labour-intensive.

155

Table 56. Costs of alternative techniques for building the Capas–Botolan road at market and shadow prices (revised estimates) (pesos)

Item Code no.	Description	Quantity	Method[1]	Man-days (M) Equipment (E)	Market price	Shadow price Low wage—high rental	Shadow price High wage—low rental
100	Clearing and grubbing	22 ha	2	M: 68	802	642	642
				E: D7	49 232	58 820	43 656
			3	M: 2 352	21 555	8 352	16 799
				E: plough, scraper	3 512	1 985	1 985
105a	Excavation (average 100 m haul)	160 000 m³	2	M: 2 078	24 267	18 202	19 641
				E: D7 grader and pneumatic roller	814 124	966 043	712 413
			3	M: 45 680	416 974	161 361	326 302
				E: wheelbarrow and steel scraper, bullcart	230 844	158 681	146 537
105b	Soft rock excavation	2 982 m³	2	M: 30	354	283	283
				E: D8 with ripper	34 350	43 710	32 190
			3	M: 4 987	48 000	18 400	37 400
				E: sledge-hammer, chisel and wheelbarrow	3 780	3 629	3 629
106	Excavation for structures	790 m³	2 and 3	M: 630	5 760	2 208	4 488
				E: —	0	0	0
110	Foundation fill	125 m³	2	M: 56	539	261	425
				E: dump-trucks and payloader	519	588	407
				M: 62	588	266	460
				E: farm tractor and trailers	745	808	586
111	Overhaul	143 000 station meter	2	M: 93	1 140	912	912
				E: dump-trucks and payloader	17 580	19 777	13 827
			3	M: 917	8 256	2 935	6 421
				E: bullcarts	7 338	3 990	3 990

			Method				
200	Borrow base (5 km)	11 100 m³		M: 617	6 965	4 318	5 689
				E: dump-trucks and payloader	62 321	73 029	50 861
			3	M: 1 337	12 377	4 931	9 609
				E: farm tractor and trailers	63 789	77 893	56 542
405	Concrete	381 m³	2 and 3	M: 1 308	13 100	6 823	10 870
				E: concrete mixer	11 416	14 096	9 350
406	Reinforcing steel	34.5 tons	2 and 3	M: 412	3 600	1 680	2 610
				E: iron cutter and bender	290	278	278
505	Reinforced concrete pipes	645 m	2 and 3	M: 3 656	32 860	18 348	27 708
				E: handtools	0	0	0
			2 and 3	Materials: concrete and steel bar	172 014	146 682	146 682
Total cost			2	Equipment, materials and labour	1 251 233	1 376 700	1 082 932
(Cost per km)					(217 228)	(339 010)	(188 009)
			3	Equipment, materials and labour	1 056 798	633 346	813 246
					(183 472)	(109 956)	(141 189)

[1] Methods: 2 = capital-intensive; 3 = modified labour-intensive.

Men or machines

Table 57. Costs of alternative techniques for building an average gravel road at market and shadow prices (*ex ante* and revised estimates) (pesos)

| Technical data | | Phase I: *ex ante* estimates | | | | Phase II: revised estimates | | |
Item code no.[1]	Quantity	Method[2]	Market prices	Shadow prices Low wage– high rental	High wage– low rental	Market prices	Shadow prices Low wage– high rental	High wage– low rental
100	3·5 ha	2	9 251	8 371	6 609	7 960	9 460	7 047
		3	7 403	7 891	6 601	3 988	1 645	2 988
105a	14 000 m³	2	84 292	101 592	75 036	73 360	86 122	64 055
		3	71 400	35 999	56 333	56 700	28 004	41 373
105b	260 m³	2	4 742	3 874	3 071	3 026	3 836	2 831
		3	3 960	2 740	3 325	4 514	1 921	3 577
106	70 m³	2	560	232	482	510	196	398
		3	473	202	409			
110	10 m³	2	100	55	58	85	68	67
		3	84	71	71	107	86	84
111	12 500 station meter	2	1 750	1 167	832	1 625	1 807	1 287
		3	729	913	639	1 375	605	909
200	1 930 m³	2	15 980	12 238	8 814	12 063	13 449	9 833
		3	18 509	15 623	15 579	13 240	13 358	11 502
405	33 m³	2 and 3	2 123[3]	1 812	1 751	2 123[3]	1 812	1 751
406	3 tons	2 and 3	338[3]	170	251	338[3]	170	251
505	56 m	2 and 3	2 853[3]	1 593	2 406	2 853[3]	1 593	2 406
Materials: cement and steel bar		2 and 3	14 937	12 737	12 737	14 937	12 737	12 737
Total cost		2	136 926	143 841	112 047	118 880	131 250	102 663
		3	122 809	79 751	100 102	100 685	62 127	77 976

[1] For explanation of code numbers, see table 56.   [2] Methods: 2 = capital-intensive; 3 = modified labour-intensive.   [3] Excludes materials.

Table 58. Costs of alternative techniques for concrete paving of roads at market and shadow prices (pesos)

| | Labour-intensive methods | | | Capital-intensive methods | | |
	Market price	Shadow prices Low wage– high rental	High wage– low rental	Market price	Shadow prices Low wage– high rental	High wage– low rental
Per m³						
Labour	5·30	3·37	4·45	4·00	2·95	3·26
Equipment	4·06	4·06	3·05	5·29	4·60	3·28
Total	9·36	7·43	7·50	9·29	7·55	6·54
Per 1 000 m³	2 153	1 709	1 725	2 137	1 737	1 504

Figure 18.   Cost data for excavating and hauling fill material by different methods at shadow prices (high wage–low rental), 0–500 m

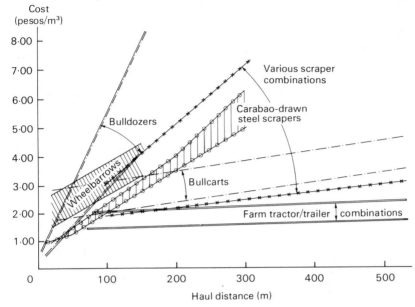

Figure 19.   Cost data for excavating and hauling fill material by different methods at shadow prices (low wage–high rental), 0–500 m

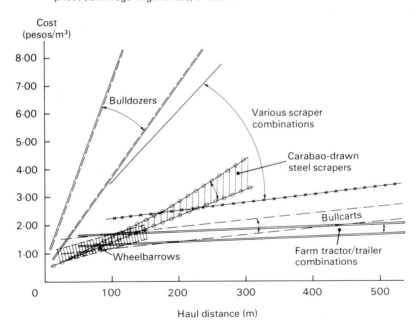

Men or machines

Table 59.   Relative social desirability of alternative methods of transport

Method of transport	Haul distance (m)	
	High wage–low rental	Low wage–high rental
Carabao-drawn cart	0–250	0–500
Farm tractor/trailer combinations	250–3 200	500 —3 400
Dump-truck/payloader	3 200+	3 400+

Figure 20.   Cost data for excavating and hauling fill material by different methods at shadow prices, 0–10 km

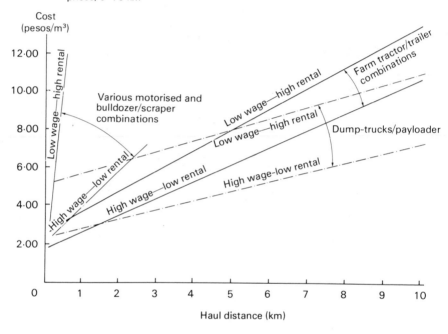

OPTIMAL TIME-INEFFICIENCY OF LABOUR-INTENSIVE TECHNIQUES

E

In this appendix we discuss the relative gestation lags of capital-intensive and labour-intensive techniques outlined in Chapter 4. Our aim is to estimate the time that can be taken on the labour-intensive technique so as to leave the net social benefits from the road exactly the same as they would have been if the road had been built more quickly by capital-intensive techniques. We make the following assumptions:

(a) k km of average gravel road can be built in a year by capital-intensive methods;

(b) this results in a benefit stream which is the equivalent of a perpetuity at accounting prices of B pesos per annum;

(c) the total accounting cost of building k km of road by capital-intensive methods is K;

(d) the total accounting cost of building the road by labour-intensive methods is L;

(e) it takes t years to build the road by labour-intensive methods; and

(f) the total cost of building the road by labour-intensive methods may be spread over time and is either:

(i) all incurred in the first year; or

(ii) equally spread over t years.

The present value of the net benefits on the capital-intensive alternative is then simply

$$PV_k = \frac{B}{\text{ARI}} - K. \tag{19}$$

The present value of the net benefits on the labour-intensive alternative is

(i) $$PV_{l_a} = \frac{1}{(1 + \text{ARI})^t} \left(\frac{B}{\text{ARI}} \right) - L; \tag{20}$$

or

(ii) $$PV_{l_b} = \frac{1}{(1 + \text{ARI})^t} \left(\frac{B}{\text{ARI}} \right) - \sum_{n=0}^{t} \frac{L/t}{(1 + \text{ARI})^n}. \tag{21}$$

We determine B from equation (19), given our assumption that the present value of the net benefits of the road, using capital-intensive methods, is just positive (using the ARI as a discount rate); hence

$$B = K \cdot \text{ARI}. \tag{22}$$

Our problem is to determine the value of t which makes $PV_l - PV_k = 0$. As from equations (19) and (22) $PV_k = 0$, the problem is to find a value for t which makes equations (20) and (21) equal to zero, given the value of the other parameters for the average gravel road in table 57. This table gives us estimates of the accounting costs per km of average gravel road with the two alternative techniques, and for the two limiting values of the shadow wages/rental ratio. We therefore need an estimate of the average length of gravel road which could be built in a year under typical Philippines conditions. The engineers estimated that, assuming a working period of nine months per year, 18·9 km of road could be built. The use of this figure yields the following total accounting cost for such a length of road with the alternative techniques for the two wage/rental ratio assumptions, and using the productivity figures from the revised estimates:

(a) cost using capital-intensive method (K) (in thousands of pesos):
  (i) $K_i = 131 \cdot 250 \times 18 \cdot 9 = 2,480 \cdot 62$ (assuming LW–HR);
  (ii) $K_{ii} = 102 \cdot 663 \times 18 \cdot 9 = 1,940 \cdot 33$ (assuming HW–LR);

(b) cost using modified labour-intensive method (L) (in thousands of pesos):
  (i) $L_i = 62 \cdot 127 \times 18 \cdot 9 = 1,174 \cdot 20$ (LW–HR);
  (ii) $L_{ii} = 77 \cdot 976 \times 18 \cdot 9 = 1,473 \cdot 746$ (HW–LR).

From (a)(i) and (a)(ii), and using our derived value of the ARI for the Philippines of 12 per cent, we can use the relationship derived above to determine the annual benefits (B) for the differing wage/rental ratio assumptions. These are as follows:

annual benefits (B) (in thousands of pesos):

  (i) $B_i = 2480 \cdot 62 \times 0 \cdot 12 = 297 \cdot 67$ (LW–HR);
  (ii) $B_{ii} = 1940 \cdot 33 = 0 \cdot 12 = 232 \cdot 833$ (HW–LR).

Substituting the above values in equations (20) and (21), we get in equation (20)

  (i) $t = 7$ years (LW–HR);
  (ii) $t = 2$ years (HW–LR);

and in equation (21)

  (i) $t = 10$ years (LW–HR);
  (ii) $t = 4$ years (HW–LR).

The particular assumptions made about the shadow wage/rental ratio and the spreading of costs on the labour-intensive method are thus crucial in deciding how relatively time-inefficient labour-intensive techniques can be and yet still be economically viable. Clearly, this is likely to be an important aspect of the choice of technique in road construction, in which both technical judgements (about the feasibility of spreading costs over time) and economic judgements (about relative shadow prices) are likely to be extremely important. Tentatively, however, our results as given above suggest that, for roads which can be built by seasonally unemployed labour, it may be desirable to use labour-intensive techniques, and even to take much longer over building the road, by building it during the agricultural slack season. This conclusion could be of some importance for rural road construction.

SELECTED BIBLIOGRAPHY

F

Allal, M.; Edmonds, G. A.: *Manual on the planning of labour-intensive road construction* (Geneva, ILO, 1977).

Atkinson, A. B.; Stiglitz, J. E.: "A new view of technological change", in *The Economic Journal* (London), Sep. 1969.

Bardhan, P. K.; Srinivasan, T. N.: "Cropsharing tenancy in agriculture: A theoretical and empirical analysis", in *The American Economic Review* (Menasha, Wis.), Mar. 1971.

Cheung, S. N. S.: "Private property rights and sharecropping", in *The Journal of Political Economy* (Chicago), Nov.-Dec. 1968.

Department of Public Works, Transportation and Communication (Philippines): *Construction of levees by labour-intensive methods* (Manila, 1972).

Dhar, P. N.; Lydall, H. F.: *The role of small enterprises in Indian economic development* (London, Asia Publishing House, 1961).

Eckaus, R. S.: "The factor proportions problem in underdeveloped areas", in *The American Economic Review*, May 1960.

Estanislao, J. P.: "A note on differential farm productivity by tenure", in *Philippine Economic Journal* (Manila), 1965, No. 1.

Harberger, A. C.: "On measuring the social opportunity cost of labour", in *International Labour Review* (Geneva), June 1971.

— : "Three basic postulates of applied welfare economics: An interpretive essay", in *The Journal of Economic Literature* (Menasha, Wis.), Sep. 1971.

Harris, J. R.: Todaro, M. P.: "Migration, unemployment and development: A two-sector analysis", in *The American Economic Review*, Mar. 1970.

Hirschman, A. O.: *The strategy of economic development* (New Haven, Conn., and London, Yale University Press, 1958).

ILO: *Sharing in development: A programme of employment, equity and growth for the Philippines* (Geneva, 1974).

Irvin, G. W., et al.: *Roads and redistribution: Social costs and benefits of labour-intensive road construction in Iran* (Geneva, ILO, 1975).

Lal, D.: "Poverty and unemployment: A question of policy", in *South Asian Review* (London), July 1972.

— : *Wells and welfare* (Paris, OECD Development Centre, 1972).

— : "Disutility of effort, migration, and the shadow wage-rate", in *Oxford Economic Papers* (Oxford), Mar. 1973.

— : "Employment, income distribution and a poverty redressal index", in *World Development* (Oxford), Mar./Apr. 1973.

— : "Adjustments for trade distortions in project analysis", in *The Journal of Development Studies* (London), Oct. 1974.

—: *Methods of project analysis: A review*, World Bank staff occasional papers, No. 16 (Baltimore and London, Johns Hopkins University Press, 1974).

Little, I. M. D.: Mirrlees, J. A.: *Social cost benefit analysis*, Vol. II of OECD: *Manual of industrial project analysis in developing countries* (Paris, 1969).

— ; — : *Project appraisal and planning for developing countries* (London, Heinemann, 1974).

McCleary, W. A., et al.: *Equipment versus employment: A social cost–benefit analysis of alternative techniques of feeder road construction in Thailand* (Geneva, ILO, 1976).

Mangahas, M.: *A broad view of the Philippine employment problem*, Discussion paper No. 72–76, 4 Dec. 1972 (Manila, University of the Philippines, School of Economics, Institute of Economic Development and Research).

— ; Encarnacion, J., Jr.: "Production submodel of the Philippine economy, 1950–69", in National Economic and Development Authority: *Econometric models of the Philippines* (Manila, 1972).

— ; Librero, A. R.: *The high-yielding varieties of rice in the Philippines: A perspective*, Discussion paper No. 73-11, 15 June 1973 (Manila, University of the Philippines, School of Economics, Institute of Economic Development and Research).

Power, J. H.; Sicat, G. P.: *The Philippines: Industrialization and trade policies* (London, Oxford University Press, 1971).

Ruttan, V. W.: "Tenure and productivity of Philippine rice-producing farms", in *Philippine Economic Journal*, 1966, No. 1.

Schumacher, E. F.: *Small is beautiful* (London, Blond & Briggs, 1973).

Scott, M. FG., et al.: *Project appraisal in practice: The Little–Mirrles method applied in Kenya* (London, Heinemann, 1976).

Sen, A. K.: *Choice of techniques* (Oxford, Blackwell, 3rd. ed., 1968).

—: *Employment, technology and development* (Oxford, Clarendon Press for the International Labour Office, 1975).

Seton, F.: *Shadow wages in the Chilean economy* (Paris, OECD Development Centre, 1972).

Takahashi, A.: *Land and peasants in Central Luzon: Socio-economic structure of a Philippine village* (Honolulu, East-West Center Press, 1970).

— : "The peasantization of *kasamá* tenants", in F. Lynch (ed.): *View from the paddy: Empirical studies of Philippine rice farming and tenancy* (Manila, Philippine Sociological Society, 1972).

UNIDO: *Guidelines for project evaluation*, Project formulation and evaluation series, No. 2 (New York, United Nations, 1972; Sales No.: E. 72. II.B.11).

United Nations, Economic Commission for Asia and the Far East: *Earthmoving by manual labour and machines*, Flood control series, No. 17 (Bangkok, 1961; Sales No.: 61.II.F.4).

Volunteers for International Technical Assistance (VITA): *Village technology handbook* (Schenectady, NY, 1970). Revised version of the earlier USAID handbook of the same name, now out of print.

Williamson, J. G.: "Capital accumulation, labor saving, and labor absorption once more", in *The Quarterly Journal of Economics* (Cambridge, Mass.), Feb. 1971.

World Bank: *Study of the substitution of labor and equipment in civil construction: Phase II final report*, Staff working paper, No. 172, 3 vols. (Washington, DC, 1974; mimeographed).